THE
ACTUALLY
DELICIOUS
AIR FRYER
COOKBOOK

Level up your air frying game
with 100 flavour-packed recipes

POPPY COOKS

THE
ACTUALLY
DELICIOUS
AIR FRYER
COOKBOOK

Photography by
Haarala Hamilton

appetite
by RANDOM HOUSE

To my mom, Vicky, who introduced
me to three of my favourite things:
TV cooking shows, champagne
and my air fryer.

Welcome to
The Actually Delicious
Air Fryer Cookbook.

My name is Poppy. I'm a 29-year-old chef from a little town called Bromsgrove, just outside of Birmingham – the UK's third biggest city and the birthplace of Ozzy Osbourne, the Chicken Tikka Masala and the Bull Ring. I started working in kitchens from the age of 17, first in a pub peeling potatoes as a kitchen assistant, juggling that job with college, and also cooking for residents at a care home while they mostly watched *The Chase*. After college I enjoyed the gastronomical wonders of fine dining in Birmingham and London, and then on to corporate catering for a bank. This was until 2020 when the whole country came to a standstill thanks to COVID-19 and all the restaurants closed their doors. I lost my job, and thinking it'd just be two weeks until things went back to normal, I started posting a few videos on what was then a relatively unknown, up-and-coming social-media platform called TikTok.

Weeks turned to months and, in the UK, the restaurant industry was still in a hard place. I had been posting my little recipe videos and content on what I eat in a day, and was over the moon to have a few videos get 10,000-ish views and to have about 4,000 followers on the platform. As fun as this new venture was – and I loved even one or two people commenting to say they tried my recipes at home – it wasn't paying the bills. In August 2020, I applied for a few jobs, including a night shift role at the frozen-food supermarket Iceland, and got rejected because I accidentally clicked the box that said I wasn't willing to work nights.

In August that year I was cooking steak and potatoes for dinner. The potatoes were little crispy cubes. Once I'd finished devouring them, I thought: 'Wow. The internet would've loved them.' So, I cooked them again and posted the video of it online. These special little potatoes became my first ever video to hit 1 million views. Fast-forward to today, somehow having over 4 million followers online, having achieved over 500 million views on my channel, meeting and working alongside my idols – Nigella Lawson, Dominique Crenn, Angela Hartnett, Giorgio Locatelli, Pierre Koffmann, Ainsley Harriott, Michel Roux Jr – to landing my dream job of being a TV cooking show judge on the BBC's *Young Masterchef*, and to my biggest achievement so far ... being a question on *The Chase*:

'Chef Poppy O'Toole rose to fame on what social media video app?'

'TikTok.'

I couldn't believe I was a question, let alone that the contestant got the answer right. Probably a guess, but I'm still chuffed. It really is a full-circle moment when I think of it on TV in the care home in Alvechurch where 17-year-old Poppy would have been serving plates of pea soup off the dinner trolley. This amazing journey brings us to me, sat here, having just finished my second recipe book. And it's all about air fryers. So, why did I write this book?

Firstly, I love my air fryer.

And that's thanks to my mom – back in 2018, just before the air-fryer hype took over the world. Funnily enough, she only bought one because the house was being renovated and she needed to cook for the family while being oven-less for a few weeks. And she was soon telling me all about how she was impressed by the speed, ease and end results. Potentially one of the earliest air-fryer converts in the country, my mom has always been a trendsetter.

Talking of my mom, one thing I've inherited from her (apart from a love of cooking) is a terrible habit of leaving the washing up until the next morning. I wish I was that person who could get everything sorted straight after dinner, clean down the table, get all the plates washed and away, and wake up to a beautiful fresh start. But even after years of working in professional kitchens, where it's so important to end the shift with a spotless kitchen, when it comes to my home life, I'm a 'worry-about-it-in-the-morning'-er.

This is where the air fryer really started to sell itself to both me and my mom. I love not having to wash up so much. Having it all cooked in the one basket. Not having trays of oil and food all over the kitchen. The air fryer really is the answer to ease and comfort in the kitchen, especially for weeknight dinners. The fewer dishes there are in the morning to sorrily clean up, regretting last night's decision and vowing to be a better person today, the better.

Ease is one thing, but I'm all about taste. The air fryer does everything an oven can do when it comes to getting the best out of your produce. Whether it's honey-glazing your carrots or lemon-roasting your chicken, there's no falling short with an air fryer when you compare it to your usual ways of cooking. Secondly, texture. And this is super-important in my line of work – you don't get the title 'Potato Queen' by accepting a soggy chip (or fries to my friends across the Pond). It was in the crisp and crunch department where the air fryer really won me over. In fact, the first thing I ever cooked in an air fryer was chips. I was expecting a quick and fairly satisfactory result, with the benefits being the time it took rather than a perfect stick of potato deliciousness. However, after the potatoes went into the air fryer RAW and cooked for only 35 minutes, I pulled out the tray, and, to my wonder, there stood a batch of perfectly cooked chips. I ate one in shock; ate a second in disbelief – and most likely ate every single one just to re-confirm that this little machine was the machine of dreams. Dreams of perfect chips.

An air fryer can get your chips closest to deep-frying – without the deep fryer. The health benefits of this are obvious, but also it's so much easier than having a big vat of oil that you somehow need to get rid of without putting it down the sink. With an air fryer you get that crisp, you get that crunch – and that's across your potatoes, your fried chicken, your pastries, or anything you might normally fry.

And if you know me, once you've won me over with the potatoes, we're friends for life. Chicken was next. It was lovely. Then a full English breakfast, one lazy (probably hungover) morning. Convenient and delicious. Then I cooked my famous crispy cube potatoes. And they were as crispy as always. I was entering my air-fryer era.

The possibilities are also endless. You can bake in an air fryer, which blew my mind. In this book are some of the most delicious cakes and desserts (I can't wait to make them again and again once I've finished writing). And who knew the air fryer was the secret to the perfect dippy egg? I need people to know how versatile this little machine can be.

My favourite things in life are simple, versatile and a little chunky. Potatoes. Pugs. Myself. My air fryer.

Another reason I wanted to write this book is because a lot of people in the culinary world turn their noses up at an air fryer. As you know, I've been a chef for 12 years now and despite an apprenticeship in a Michelin-starred restaurant and working my way up through fine dining in Birmingham and London, it was my time working in the care-home kitchen that actually established my view of good food. It can be fancy, perhaps – but it definitely has to be easy and accessible to all. Yes, I was only making cottage pie (minced/ground beef topped with mashed potato and baked – a simple, yet delicious British classic), but I saw first-hand how easy, simple food is so important; how it can still be delicious enough to be the highlight of someone's day. The care-home residents didn't want a jus splashed across the plate with foams and deconstructed dishes served over a 20-plate tasting menu. They wanted real, delicious, hearty food and I loved being able to provide that. I'm proud to have all the skills that I learned in fine dining while still having a love for everyday delicious cooking.

This is where some in the culinary world might look down on our friend, the air fryer. They might see it as a bit of a fad, a lazy option for quick results. They might say there's no way they'd have it in the kitchen – like they wouldn't have a microwave. Well, don't worry kids. This is a judgement-free zone and I'm partial to a ping in the microwave when time calls for it.

That's the thing. Good food needs to also be about accessibility and convenience. As a chef, I know that millions of people are at home using an air fryer, so I want to teach them how to get the most out of the food they're cooking every day. Because it can be actually delicious!

Finally, I wanted to write this book because there's no other book like it. I love cookbooks. They're my biggest form of inspiration. I don't really watch cooking videos on YouTube or read recipes on websites. If I'm struggling to think of what to cook, I love to sprawl my favourite recipe books across the floor and just read pages and pages. And I've already told you about how I was converted to the air fryer, so hand-in-hand came the time where I was looking for an air-fryer cookbook to spark some new ideas for what to cook. After scrolling online at the selection of books out there, I realised the lack of variety. Most of what I could find looked like an instruction manual. Clunky infographics, like something I'd use to build some Ikea furniture. There was nothing like the cookbooks I'm used to – full of delicious food and easy-to-follow recipes while looking sleek and appetising.

The idea was born ... it was time to make
The Actually Delicious Air Fryer Cookbook.

MEAT

CHICKEN WINGS

If I hadn't followed the path of a potato obsession, I think I may have gone for chicken wings. I love how versatile they are. A different sauce or flavour topping and you've got a whole different dish each time. Like potatoes, you can get messy with them, dunk them, lick your fingers and eat endless amounts. That's the food I'm down for. Wings in the air fryer make sense because it's efficient, there's no mess and the results are just how you'd want your wings to turn out. Flavoursome on the outside and succulent on the inside, this recipe comes with my three favourite ways to eat chicken wings. Pick your favourite of my favourites and enjoy!

1   Heat your air fryer to 190°C/375°F.

2   Mix together the flour and all the spices and the salt in a mixing bowl, to get everything incorporated. Tip the wing pieces into the flour mixture and give them a good toss.

3   Give your air-fryer basket a little spray with some oil.

4   Dust of any excess flour from your wings and place them in the air-fryer basket (for optimum deliciousness, do this in batches of up to 10 wings at a time, depending on the size of your air fryer) and cook for 15 minutes, until golden and cooked through.

5   Either enjoy them plain and crispy or try one of the saucy variations below. Just toss your cooked wings in the sauce of your choice.

MY SUGGESTIONS

Buffalo hot sauce: Simple yet effective – combine half a bottle of (Frank's) hot sauce with 20g/1 tablespoon of butter and 1 teaspoon of runny honey. Heat it up until melted together, then toss your wings in the sauce. Voilà!

Sticky sweet soy sauce: Get a pan. Bring to the boil 2 tablespoons of dark soy sauce, 1 tablespoon of runny honey, 1 teaspoon of rice wine vinegar, 1 finely grated garlic clove, 1 teaspoon of finely grated fresh ginger and 1 tablespoon of tomato ketchup. Once boiling, remove from the heat, do a taste test, adjust as you fancy, and once you're happy, toss them wings in.

Lemon and black pepper: Grab 1 lemon, zested and juiced, 1 teaspoon of cracked black pepper and 20–30g/1–2 tablespoons of melted butter. Mix the lemon zest, black pepper and butter together, then add 1 teaspoon of lemon juice at a time until you are happy with the sourness. Season with salt and toss them wings.

Serves as many as you have wings for

100–200g/¾–1⅔ cups plain/all purpose flour (depending on how many wings)
1 teaspoon smoked paprika
1 teaspoon garlic powder
1 teaspoon ground coriander
1 teaspoon cayenne pepper
2 teaspoons salt
6–10 chicken wings per person, separated into drums and flats
vegetable oil, for spraying

WHOLE CHICKEN

My mind was blown when I first cooked a WHOLE chicken in the air fryer. Once you try it, you'll be going back again and again. This is an easy but beautiful dish to enjoy as a Sunday roast or midweek supper. Save extras for sandwiches.

1 Pat the chicken dry with kitchen paper and season generously with table salt.

2 Make a flavoured butter by mixing the softened butter with the finely chopped garlic, thyme, rosemary and lemon zest and season with salt and ground black pepper.

3 Heat the air fryer to 190°C/375°F.

4 Using your fingers, prise open the skin on the breast and slide the flavoured butter inside, squishing it around to spread it out underneath the skin a little. Pop the zested half-lemon, reserved thyme stalks and whole garlic cloves inside the cavity of the chicken, then drizzle the skin with olive oil and sprinkle with a good grind of black pepper. Place the chicken in the air-fryer basket and cook for 45–50 minutes, until the juices run clear.

MY SUGGESTIONS

The flavoured butter used here is my go-to! But there are so many ways to add flavour to your air-fryer bird. Try experimenting with different herbs, spices and acids. For a tarragon butter, use 3 tarragon sprigs (stalks and all). Get them finely chopped and add them to softened butter, with finely chopped garlic and half a finely chopped banana shallot. Season with salt and black pepper.

For peri-peri flavour, deseed a large red pepper and grab a quartered red onion, 1 garlic bulb (whole with just the top cut off) and 2 red chillies. Put in the air fryer at 200°C/400°F with some olive oil and salt, and roast for 20 minutes. Squeeze out the garlic flesh and get everything in a blender, then blend. Add the zest and juice of 1 lemon, 2 oregano sprigs, 2 teaspoons of smoked paprika, a pinch of salt and 1 teaspoon of red wine vinegar, and give it a good mix. Get this in a saucepan and cook on low for 20 minutes, until thickened, then blend while drizzling in 100ml/7 tablespoons of olive oil, until thick and smooth. Leave to cool and then add at least 2 tablespoons of this to the softened butter and use as above. Halfway through cooking the chicken, brush over some more of the sauce for extra flavour.

**Serves 6
(or 4 with leftovers)**

1.6kg/3½lb whole chicken, brought to room temperature (which will take about an hour)
40g/3 tablespoons butter, softened
6 garlic cloves, 3 finely chopped, 3 whole
4 thyme sprigs, leaves chopped, stalks reserved
2 rosemary sprigs, leaves chopped
½ lemon, zested
2 tablespoons olive oil
salt and ground black pepper

CRISPY THIGHS AND DRUMSTICKS

You can't beat crispy, crispy chicken thighs and drumsticks. Plot twist – I also enjoy a cold bit of thigh the next day, straight out of the fridge and straight into my mouth. Enjoy as you please.

1   Heat the air fryer to 200°C/400°F.

2   Season the chicken thighs or drumsticks generously with table salt.

3   Drizzle the chicken thighs with the oil and place them in the air-fryer basket. Cook for 25–30 minutes, until the skin is crisp and golden.

Serves 4

4–8 chicken thighs or drumsticks, at room temperature
2 tablespoons vegetable oil
salt and ground black pepper

MY SUGGESTIONS

For the simplest, most delicious dinner, I'd just serve these gorgeous thighs and drumsticks with a side salad or green veg, my crispy cube potatoes (see page 120) and shavings of Parmesan. Delicious!

Or, why not try tandoori-spice-rub chicken pieces, served with rice and cucumber tomato salad. In a bowl, mix 2 tablespoons of tandoori spice mix with the juice of a lemon, a drizzle of olive oil and some salt. Add the chicken pieces and rub all over, then leave to marinate for 20 minutes. Cook according to the recipe. In the meantime, chop two-thirds of a cucumber into 1cm/½-inch cubes, get 100g/⅔ cups of cherry tomatoes chopped into quarters and mix in 1 teaspoon of mint sauce (the one from the supermarket). Season and set aside. Gather enough cooked rice for each person and get a large frying pan on a medium heat. Add in 4 tablespoons of butter, 1 chopped onion, 2 chopped garlic cloves, 1 teaspoon of mustard seeds and 2 dried chillies. Cook until the onion is golden. Then add the rice and mix well. Season with 2 teaspoons of garam masala and serve with the rest of the meal.

Another of my favourites is orange soy chicken glaze. Mix together the zest and juice of 2 oranges, 6 tablespoons of runny honey, 3 tablespoons of dark soy sauce, 2 tablespoons of hot sauce (or more depending on your taste), 3 tablespoons of rice vinegar, 1 tablespoon of garlic and ginger paste (or 2 minced garlic cloves) and 1cm/½-inch piece of fresh ginger (grated). Add your chicken pieces to the glaze and leave to marinate for a minimum of 30 minutes. Cook the chicken according to the recipe but brush with the glaze every 5–10 minutes. With the remaining glaze, get it in a saucepan and bring it to the boil, then let it cook and reduce. Serve with broccoli (see page 140), cooked rice and some sugar snap peas, drizzled in the glaze.

CHICKEN TENDERS AND NUGGETS

I was always a kid who would show off that she'd eat with the adults and eat whatever they were eating, whether that was a fillet of fish, seafood or some raw beef, because I was such a 'grown up'. In reality, I was trying to be cool. That meant part of me loved going round to a friend's house after school to enjoy the classics like nuggets, turkey twizzlers or potato smilies. So this dish is dedicated to Steph, Martha's mom, who was always there to feed my nugget needs, mostly due to what can now be considered as Martha's childhood addiction to chicken nuggets.

1   Trim any sinew from the chicken mini fillets, season generously and pour over the buttermilk (or milk/lemon mixture). Marinate in the fridge for at least 2 hours, or overnight if you can.

2   Heat the air fryer to 220°C/425°F (or your air fryer's maximum temperature).

3   Find three shallow bowls. Crack the eggs into one bowl and whisk gently. Add the flour to the second bowl and the breadcrumbs to the third. Lightly season the breadcrumbs.

4   Using one hand for the wet ingredients (eggs) and the other for the dry ingredients (flour and breadcrumbs), toss each piece of chicken in the flour, then the egg, then the breadcrumbs, to coat fully, and place the pieces on a lined baking tray.

5   Lightly spray your breaded chicken with oil and get them into the air-fryer basket, leaving plenty of space between each (you might need to do this in batches, depending on the size of your air fryer). Cook for 10-12 minutes, turning halfway through, until crisp and golden.

Serves 4

640g/1½lb chicken mini fillets
400ml/1⅔ cups buttermilk (or 500ml/2 cups whole milk mixed with the juice of 1 lemon and left to stand for 10 minutes)
2 eggs
50g/heaping ⅓ cup plain/all purpose flour
100g/2 cups Panko breadcrumbs
vegetable oil, for spraying
salt and ground black pepper

MY SUGGESTIONS

Get your friends together with a platter of these, mozzarella dippers (see page 167), onion rings (see page 156), potato skins (see page 122), chips (see page 113) and plenty of dips. Enjoy!

Turn these into chicken nuggets if you prefer. Serve up with chips and salad, or even ... plot twist ... load them up in a sandwich or baguette for my ultimate guilty pleasure! Swap the chicken tenders for 400g/14oz of chicken breast, trimming and cutting it into about 4cm/1½-inch bite-sized pieces. And use 250ml/1 cup of whole milk rather than the buttermilk to marinate. Coat the pieces in the egg, flour and breadcrumbs as for the tenders, then cook them in the air-fryer basket, spaced apart, for 8-10 minutes, turning halfway through (and in batches, if necessary), until crisp and golden.

SALT AND PEPPER CHICKEN BITES

Fakeaways really came to the forefront in lockdown as everyone was craving their local treat made at home. From this, I've taken to having a 'fakeaway night' as a bit of a treat. I'm talking a full spread of all your favourite takeaway items, made at home, without breaking the bank. Leading with this salt and pepper chicken is a must!

1   Heat the air fryer to 200°C/400°F.

2   Mix the flour and five-spice together in a large bowl. Add the chicken pieces and toss to coat well.

3   Get your chicken pieces into the hot air-fryer basket, making sure that you leave a little room in between each piece, and spray over your oil (do this in batches, depending on the size of your air fryer).

4   Cook for 5 minutes, then give the pieces a good toss, and add the chopped peppers, sliced onion and chilli and cook for a further 7–10 minutes, until everything is cooked.

MY SUGGESTIONS

One to serve up as part of a Chinese fakeaway feast. Think of these beautiful bites alongside your lemon chicken (see page 31), spring rolls (see page 154), prawn toast (see page 104), wontons (see page 160) and some rice on the side. Invite me around as well, please!

Serves 4

2 tablespoons plain/all purpose flour
1 teaspoon Chinese five-spice
4 skinless, boneless chicken breasts, cut into 4cm/1½-inch bite-sized pieces
vegetable oil, for spraying
2 green peppers, deseeded and cut into bite-sized pieces
1 onion, sliced
1 red chilli, deseeded and sliced

LEMON AND HONEY CHICKEN SKEWERS

There are no better friends for chicken than deliciously sweet honey and the tangy, tasty twang of lemon cutting through. Serve this up on a bed of fresh salad, with your pasta of choice, or even on a crusty baguette, and you'll be in chicken heaven. BRB I'm going to make a honey lemon chicken baguette right now.

1   Mix the lemon zest and juice, garlic, honey, chilli flakes, sea salt, olive oil, crushed peppercorns, rosemary and thyme together in a bowl.

2   Add the chicken chunks and stir to coat the chicken all over. Cover the bowl and leave the chicken in the fridge to marinate for 1 hour. (This is a good time to get your skewers soaking if you haven't already.)

3   Remove the chicken from the fridge and leave it for about 30 minutes to come up to room temperature.

4   Heat the air fryer to 180°C/350°F.

5   Thread your chicken pieces on to the skewers and cook for 8–10 minutes, until the chicken is golden brown and cooked through, brushing with honey every now and then.

MY SUGGESTIONS

These are really delicious with roast potatoes (see page 119), a side salad and a feta dressing. To make the dressing: in a blender add 100g/1 cup of crumbled feta, 1 tablespoon of Greek yogurt, the juice of half a lemon (more to taste if you like it lemony), and black pepper. Get the blender going and, while it's on, drizzle in olive oil until you have a mayonnaise consistency.

The fact that these are delicious in a baguette is even more of a reason to make them. You just need some baguette (what a surprise), mayo, rocket and crispy streaky bacon. Just make larger batches and keep in the fridge for up to 3 days.

It can also top pasta; make yourself a little lemon alfredo! Just boil up your fave pasta shape, and in a separate pan add some double/ heavy cream, lemon zest, squeeze of lemon juice and plenty of black pepper, and bring to a boil. Add in the pasta and chicken pieces and cook for a few minutes until combined and saucy. Serve with some garlic bread from page 168.

Serves 4

1 lemon, zested and juiced
½ garlic bulb, cloves finely chopped
2 tablespoons runny honey, plus extra for brushing
1 tablespoon chilli flakes
1 tablespoon sea-salt flakes
1 tablespoon olive oil
1 teaspoon black peppercorns, crushed
2 rosemary sprigs, leaves picked
4 thyme sprigs, leaves picked
4 skinless, boneless chicken breasts, cut into 3cm/1¼-inch dice

You will also need
8 wooden skewers, soaked for 1 hour in hot water

LEMON CHICKEN

I love this dish, especially on a Saturday night when you've got friends round to enjoy with a few beers and a good ol' trashy movie on the TV. If anyone wants to come over next weekend to join the lemon chicken party, give me a bell.

1   Get all the marinade ingredients into a large mixing bowl or tray large enough to fit all the chicken, and mix well. Add in the chicken breasts so that they are submerged, then cover and leave to marinate in the fridge for at least 1 hour, but ideally overnight.

2   Bring the chicken back to room temperature before you cook – it will need about 30 minutes or so out of the fridge. When you're ready, mix the crust ingredients together in a bowl.

3   Heat the air fryer to 190°C/375°F.

4   One by one, take the chicken breasts out of the buttermilk marinade and dredge them in the crust mixture, dusting off any excess, then place them straight into your air-fryer basket (add as many as fit comfortably, depending on the size of your air fryer).

5   Spray the chicken and the basket liberally with oil and cook for 30 minutes, then turn over the chicken breasts and cook for a further 10–15 minutes, until crispy and golden.

6   While the chicken is cooking, make your lemony sauce. Put the lemon juice, honey, chicken stock and soy sauce into a saucepan over a medium heat. Bring to the boil.

7   Mix the cornflour with a touch of water to make a slurry and then whisk this into your boiling lemon sauce to thicken.

8   Once the sauce has thickened to the consistency you like, turn the heat down to low and keep it warm while the chicken finishes cooking. Just before the chicken is done, stir in the butter to give the sauce a lovely shiny and luxurious texture. Serve up with the chicken and enjoy.

MY SUGGESTIONS

Make a sticky rice (use the packet instructions or even ping it in the microwave – we don't judge in this household!) and flavour with some fresh coriander/cilantro, the zest of a lemon and some pan-fried pak choi for health.

Serves 4

4 skin-on, boneless chicken breasts
vegetable oil

For the marinade
500ml/2 cups buttermilk (or 500ml/2 cups whole milk mixed with the juice of 1 lemon and left to stand for 10 minutes)
1 lemon, juiced
1 tablespoon paprika
1 tablespoon garlic powder
1 tablespoon ground white pepper
1 tablespoon salt

For the crust
100g/heaping ¾ cup plain/all purpose flour
50g/½ cup Parmesan, finely grated
1 teaspoon paprika
1 teaspoon garlic powder
salt and ground black pepper

For the sauce
4 lemons, juiced
3 tablespoons honey
100ml/7 tablespoons chicken stock
1 teaspoon dark soy sauce
1 tablespoon cornflour/ cornstarch, or more if needed
couple of knobs of butter

CHICKEN BURGERS

Are you a chicken burger or a beef burger kinda person? If I had to pick a team, it'd be a chicken burger. Without suggesting I frequent a fast-food outlet at least once a week ['nervous laugh'], it's always a chicken burger I go for. Layer up and enjoy!

1   Trim any sinew from the chicken thighs, season generously and pour over the buttermilk (or milk/lemon mixture). Marinate in the fridge for at least 2 hours, or overnight if you can.

2   Heat the air fryer to 220°C/425°F (or your air fryer's maximum temperature).

3   Find three shallow bowls. Crack the eggs into one bowl and whisk gently. Add the flour to the second bowl and the breadcrumbs to the third. Lightly season the breadcrumbs.

4   Using one hand for the wet ingredients (eggs) and the other for the dry ingredients (flour and breadcrumbs), toss each piece of chicken in the flour, then the egg, then the breadcrumbs. Repeat the process for a second time, until the pieces are fully coated, and place them on a lined baking tray.

5   Lightly drizzle or spray the breaded chicken with olive oil and add the thighs to the air-fryer basket, leaving plenty of space between each piece (you may need to do this in batches). Cook for 10–12 minutes, turning halfway through, until crisp and golden.

Serves 4

320g/12oz skinless, boneless chicken thighs
400ml/1⅔ cups buttermilk (or 500ml/2 cups whole milk mixed with the juice of 1 lemon and left to stand for 10 minutes)
2 eggs
50g/heaping ⅓ cup plain/all purpose flour
100g/2 cups Panko breadcrumbs
olive oil, for spraying
salt and ground black pepper

MY SUGGESTIONS

I like to serve these tasty chicken burgers in a classic or brioche bun, loaded with burger sauce, tomatoes and lettuce; always remember to toast your buns before serving!

Mix it up with a chicken Caesar burger: simply layer the bun with romaine lettuce, your chicken burger, crispy bacon, a few shavings of Parmesan and lashings of Caesar dressing. If you want to make the dressing: in a bowl, mix 5 chopped anchovies (optional), 2 tablespoons of chopped capers, 4 tablespoons of finely grated Parmesan, the juice of a lemon, a pinch of salt, plenty of black pepper and 3–5 tablespoons of mayonnaise. (This is a cheat's Caesar dressing, by the way – but I'm not telling.)

One of my favourites is a buffalo chicken burger. Coat your burger in buffalo hot sauce straight out of the air fryer, and layer up your bun with shredded iceberg lettuce, pickles and blue cheese sauce.

STUFFED CHICKEN BREASTS

Another revelation in the air fryer is stuffing your breasts and getting them straight in, which makes for a tasty dinner option, especially on a weeknight when you're after something quick and easy. It's a good one to mix up with different flavours in the stuffing – choose your favourites and let me know how delicious they are.

1   Heat the air fryer to 200°C/400°F.

2   Using a sharp knife, carefully make a pocket in the fattest top part of each chicken breast.

3   Mix the cream cheese and pesto together and use the mixture to fill the pockets in the chicken breasts. This can get a bit messy, but get those breasts stuffed as best you can.

4   Season the chicken breasts lightly with salt and pepper, then wrap a slice of Parma ham around each breast.

5   Place the stuffed and wrapped breasts in the air-fryer basket and cook for 15 minutes, until golden and cooked through.

MY SUGGESTIONS

I like to serve these with baby potatoes, asparagus, peas and a bit of garlic butter, or quite simply on a bed of fresh salad for a light lunch.

Mix it up with sun-dried tomato pesto with the cream cheese for a beautiful tomatoey twist.

Or try stuffing your chicken with around 4 tablespoons of soft goat's cheese, 1 tablespoon of runny honey, 4 grated garlic cloves and plenty of black pepper for a gorgeously stuffed breast.

Serves 4

4 skinless, boneless chicken breasts
4 tablespoons full-fat cream cheese
2 tablespoons basil pesto
4 slices of Parma ham
salt and ground black pepper

CHICKEN THIGH GYROS

This might just be one of my all-time favourite dinners. I love chicken gyros. Unfortunately, I cannot ever pronounce it correctly (it's 'yee-ros' not 'jiy-roes'), but one thing I can do is enjoy this dinner again and again – they are a staple on my weekly dinners list for the foreseeable.

1   Get all of your ingredients in a big bowl and mix them up, making sure the chicken is well coated. Cover and leave in the fridge for at least 1 hour, but overnight if you can. Take the chicken out of the fridge for about 15–30 minutes to start to come up to room temperature before you cook.

2   Heat the air fryer to 170°C/340°F.

3   Thread the chicken pieces on to the skewers, one on top of another, and slather them with any marinade that's left in the bowl.

4   Place the kebabs in the air-fryer basket and loosely cover with some foil, cook for 25 minutes, then remove the foil. Baste the kebabs with any juices that have collected in the bottom of the basket and increase the temperature to 200°C/400°F. Cook for a further 5–10 minutes to get some colour of the outside of the chicken thighs.

MY SUGGESTIONS

Once the kebabs are ready, serve with flatbreads, chips, a bit of garlic mayo, salad and pickled red cabbage. Easy and classic. Or try serving with cooked spiced rice, jarred peppers, crumbled feta and tossed salad.

These gyros are also perfect for lunches – in wraps, on salads, on grains, and just as they are.

Serves 2

4–6 skinless, boneless chicken thighs, cut into quarters
3 tablespoons Greek yogurt
2 teaspoons ground cumin
2 teaspoons ground coriander
2 teaspoons smoked paprika
1 teaspoon ground cinnamon
2 teaspoons chilli flakes
1 teaspoon sea-salt flakes
a good twist of black pepper
½ lemon, juiced
drizzle of olive oil

You will also need
4 wooden skewers, soaked in hot water for 1 hour

TURKEY CROWN

If you're reading this, Merry Christmas, or hope you're having a great Thanksgiving. People hardly ever seem to have turkey out of season. On the off-chance it's neither Christmas nor Thanksgiving, and actually you are, well done you for doing something a bit different. People say turkey is bland, and I say you're just cooking it wrong. Try this way and enjoy a whole new chapter of turkey-loving in your life.

1   Mix your dry brine ingredients and sprinkle 1 tablespoon of it on the inside of the turkey crown carcass. Use the rest in between the skin and the flesh. Leave the crown in the fridge to brine for at least 1 day.

2   When you're ready to cook, bring the turkey up to room temperature (about 1 hour).

3   Heat the air fryer to 170°C/340°F. Use your fingers to prise open the skin and push the softened butter inside, squishing out underneath the skin. Drizzle with the oil and cover loosely with a piece of greaseproof paper and a piece of foil.

4   Sit the turkey crown in the air-fryer basket and cook for 30 minutes. Remove the greaseproof and foil and cook for another 30–40 minutes, until golden and the juices run clear. Remove the turkey from the air fryer, cover and leave to rest for at least 20 minutes before carving.

MY SUGGESTIONS

You know the deal with this one: whether it's Christmas, Thanksgiving or just any day of the year you fancy a turkey roast, serve this up with your choice of air-fryer potato dishes (roast potatoes, page 119; hasselbacks, page 114; crispy potato cubes, page 130; wedges, page 121; chips, page 113; or even mashed potato, page 83), and a selection of carrots (see page 139), parsnips (see page 130), sprouts (see page 136), broccoli (see page 140), asparagus (see page 131) or shredded cabbage.

Serves 4–6

1.25kg/2¾lb turkey
   crown
50g/3 tablespoons
   butter, softened
1 tablespoon
   vegetable oil

For the dry brine
2 tablespoons sea-salt
   flakes
1 tablespoon dark brown
   soft sugar
1 teaspoon dried thyme
1 teaspoon ground
   mixed spice
2 rosemary sprigs,
   leaves finely chopped

BREADED TURKEY STEAKS

I'm on the turkey-loving train as it's a cheaper option and can be equally delicious as your usual chicken. Bread up your turkey steaks and fall in love with turkey as much as I do.

1 Sandwich the turkey steaks in between two pieces of greaseproof paper and bash them with a rolling pin to flatten them. Season the meat generously, place the breasts in a bowl and pour over the buttermilk (or milk/lemon mixture). Marinate in the fridge for at least 2 hours, or overnight if you can.

2 Heat the air fryer to 220°C/425°F (or your air fryer's maximum temperature).

3 Find three shallow bowls. Crack the eggs into one bowl and whisk gently. Add the flour to the second bowl and the breadcrumbs to the third. Lightly season the breadcrumbs.

4 Using one hand for the wet ingredients (eggs) and the other for the dry ingredients (flour and breadcrumbs), gently dip each turkey breast in the flour, then the egg, then the breadcrumbs to coat fully, and place the breasts on a lined baking tray.

5 Spray the breaded turkey with oil and get it in the air-fryer basket, leaving plenty of space between each piece (do this in batches, depending on the size of your air fryer). Cook for 10–12 minutes, turning halfway through, until crisp and golden.

Serves 4

4 turkey breast steaks (about 500g/1lb total)
500ml/2 cups buttermilk (or 500ml/2 cups whole milk mixed with the juice of 1 lemon and left to stand for 10 minutes)
2 eggs
50g/heaping ⅓ cup plain/all purpose flour
100g/2 cups Panko breadcrumbs
vegetable oil, for spraying
salt and ground black pepper

MY SUGGESTIONS

The possibilities are endless here. You can burger it up, or treat yourself by topping it with mozzarella, cutting it up and serving it atop a bed of tomato pasta.

Level up by flavouring your breadcrumbs with grated Parmesan, chopped rosemary leaves and black pepper.

SPICED TURKEY KEBABS

A delicious take on the kebab that is much easier to rustle up this way than it would be firing up the BBQ. Turkey is a great alternative for other mince as it's often cheaper, is a healthier option and cooks up nicely in the air fryer. Easy to make and always a crowd pleaser.

1 Put all your ingredients, except the vegetable oil, in a mixing bowl, season with salt and pepper, and give them a good mix together so that they are thoroughly combined.

2 Heat a small frying pan over a medium heat and drop in a little taster of the mixture – fry it off and give it a try just to make sure you are happy with the seasoning. Adjust the mixture if necessary.

3 Heat the air fryer to 200°C/400°F.

4 Once you like what you're tasting, mould equal portions of the minced meat around the soaked skewers to get that kebab look. Once all the kebabs are made up, add them to the air-fryer basket (they can go on top of each other as you're going to turn them anyway).

5 Give them a good spray with oil and then cook them for 10 minutes, turning them halfway through, until they are golden all over and cooked through.

MY SUGGESTIONS

Delicious with pittas, fresh tomatoes and cucumber salad, pickles, chillies – and some chips on the side, of course! Add a bit of grated garlic to your mayo. Or, if you're fancying going bread-free, dish this one up with spiced couscous, grilled aubergine/eggplant, tahini and pomegranate.

Serves 4

500g/about 1lb turkey mince/ground turkey
1 red onion, finely chopped
2 garlic cloves, crushed
2 teaspoons smoked paprika
2 teaspoons ground cumin
2 teaspoons ground coriander
15g/⅓ cup flat-leaf parsley, leaves and stems chopped
vegetable oil, for spraying
salt and ground black pepper

You will also need
8 wooden skewers, soaked for 1 hour in hot water

AROMATIC CRISPY DUCK

The ultimate sharer – every crowd will be full of people fighting over the last pancake when these come out on the dinner table. They are cute and fun to eat, and the perfect size that you can happily eat eight to yourself. Oops! I mean a sensible two to three!

1   Heat the air fryer to 150°C/300°F.

2   Add the Sichuan peppercorns to a small frying pan set over a medium heat, and toast for 30 seconds, until fragrant. Tip the peppercorns into a mortar and crush them with a pestle. Add the Chinese five-spice, stir to combine, and season with salt and pepper.

3   Rub the spice mixture over the skin of the duck and inside the cavity. Tuck the garlic and ginger inside the cavity, too.

4   Place the duck in the air-fryer basket and cook for 2½–3 hours, until the leg meat pulls away from the bone and the skin is crisp. You'll need to drain the fat from the tray at the bottom of the air fryer frequently, so pour it into a glass jar – and use it to make unreal roast potatoes.

5   If the skin isn't crisp enough after the cooking time, increase the temperature to 200°C/400°F and cook for a further 30 minutes, until it's perfect.

Serves 4

1 teaspoon Sichuan peppercorns
1 tablespoon Chinese five-spice
4 garlic cloves, peeled and bruised
30g/2-inch piece fresh ginger, finely sliced (no need to peel)
1 whole duck, about 1.75kg/3¾lb
salt and ground black pepper

MY SUGGESTIONS

Serve with 8–12 ready-made Chinese-style pancakes, with finely sliced spring onion, half a cucumber cut into matchsticks, and a good load of hoisin or sweet chilli sauce. Get wrapping to your heart's content. You could start this meal off with some wontons (see page 160) and prawn toast (see page 104), if you like.

Try this with 4 duck legs, rather than a whole duck. Use the same quantity of spice mix, but cook for 30–45 minutes, and crisp up for 15 minutes.

BACON

I don't need to write a paragraph here to tell you just how much I love bacon. If I had to write a love letter to a food, it would probably be to bacon (other than potatoes, of course). Bacon, I love you.

1   Heat the air fryer to 200°C/400°F.

2   Get the bacon in the air-fryer basket, leaving plenty of space between each piece. For the streaky bacon, cook for 6–7 minutes; or for the back bacon cook for 8–9 minutes, turning halfway through, until crisp and golden (do this in batches, depending on the size of your air fryer).

Serves 4

8 rashers of streaky or back bacon

SAUSAGES

I trained for a decade in professional restaurants so that I could now teach you how to air-fry a sausage. If my life is worth one thing, please go on and enjoy said sausage.

1   Heat the air fryer to 200°C/400°F.

2   Get the sausages in the air-fryer basket and cook for 15 minutes, turning once or twice, until golden (you might have to do this in batches, depending on the size of your air fryer).

Serves 4

8 pork sausages

MY SUGGESTIONS

Another classic for either breakfast or a sandwich, or pile these bad boys up with plenty of mashed potato (see page 83) and onion gravy.

For an onion gravy, slice up 3 onions. Get them in a saucepan with a knob of butter on a medium–high heat. Add some thyme and rosemary leaves for extra flavour and season well with salt and pepper. Fry until coloured and golden, then add plain/all purpose flour, a spoonful at a time, constantly mixing until a doughy paste forms (you will probably need only 2–3 tablespoons of flour). Then, have 500ml/2 cups of beef stock warming up and bit by bit add the stock to the onions and cook out until thickened. This is the simplest of gravy options and works so well with bangers.

WHOLE CHUNK OF HONEY-GLAZED GOCHUJANG BACON

You need to cook your bacon whole at least once in your life. It's surprisingly easy, gives the option for extra flavour when you come to slice it up, and is often more cost effective. It's as simple as throwing your bacon in the air fryer, adding those flavours and basting your beauty until it's decadently red and delicious.

1 Mix the gochujang and honey together in a small bowl, ready to slather over the bacon.

2 Heat the air fryer to 180°C/350°F.

3 Put the slab of bacon in the liner (if the bacon is too big, just cut it in half), pour the honey and gochujang mixture over the bacon slab and get it in the air-fryer basket.

4 Cook the bacon for 30–50 minutes, basting every 10 minutes so that the glaze sticks to the bacon, until cooked through.

5 Remove from the air fryer and carve up.

MY SUGGESTIONS

Go family-style and get your big lump of meat on the table for everyone to enjoy, with sharing bowls of air-fryer grilled spring onions (see page 131), honey roast carrots (see page 139), crispy kale (see page 129) and a potato of your choice (see pages 110–126 for my potato recipes).

Or slice up that bacon and keep it in the fridge for snacking, sandwiches, salads or soups. Heat up slices by air-frying at 180°C/350°F for 5–10 minutes before eating.

If you're not a fan of spice, leave out the gochujang and just go for a honey-glazed piece of bacon, or try maple syrup for woodier glaze.

Serves 4

2 tablespoons gochujang paste
100g/⅓ cup runny honey
500g/about 1lb whole slab of smoked streaky bacon, rind removed (ask your butcher to get this for you)

You will also need
silicone or parchment liner that fits inside your air fryer

SAUSAGE PATTIES

Ba-ba-ba-ba-bah ... I'm loving these! This one is dedicated to everyone's favourite fast-food clown, who I now ask kindly to not sue me. Enjoy a brunch of these beauties for the ultimate hangover cure!

1 Warm a small frying pan over a medium heat. Add the fennel seeds and toast for 30 seconds, until fragrant. Tip the seeds into a mortar and roughly crush with a pestle.

2 Tip the pork mince into a large bowl and add the crushed toasted fennel seeds, along with the sage, thyme, cayenne pepper, nigella seeds, salt and pepper. Marinate the pork in the fridge for at least 1 hour, or overnight if you can.

3 About an hour before you intend to cook, remove the pork mixture from the fridge and leave it to come up to room temperature. Heat the air fryer to 220°C/425°F (or your air fryer's maximum temperature).

4 Roll a piece of pork mixture into a ball, just larger than a golf ball, then flatten it into a patty with the palm of your hand. Repeat with the remaining mixture, until you have 8 patties.

5 Brush each side of the patties with a little olive oil and get them in the air-fryer basket, making sure there is plenty of space between each (for optimum deliciousness do this in batches, depending on the size of your air fryer).

6 Cook for 8–10 minutes, turning halfway through, until cooked through with deliciously crisp edges. Set aside to rest for a few minutes before serving.

MY SUGGESTIONS

Inspired by those fast-food Golden Arches, have these patties on an English muffin, with a slice of American cheese and a fried egg. Or, you could make this with a pan-poached egg: get a large frying pan on to a medium heat and add a splash of cooking oil. Then, using a large, round, oiled cookie cutter in the pan, crack the egg inside the cookie cutter to make that well-known shape. Add a few tablespoons of boiling water to the outside of the cookie cutter and then put a lid on the pan. Leave to cook for a few minutes and then you should have a pan-poached round egg.

Serves 4

1 teaspoon fennel seeds
500g/about 1lb pork mince/ground pork
4 sage leaves, finely chopped
4 thyme sprigs, leaves finely chopped
¼ teaspoon cayenne pepper
1 teaspoon nigella seeds
1 teaspoon sea-salt flakes
a generous amount of ground black pepper
olive oil, for brushing

PORCHETTA

A pork dish for when you want to push the boat out for an extra-special dinner, made much easier with your air fryer. This one takes a bit longer but as always, is 1,000% worth the wait. Treat yourself this Sunday.

1   Prep your pork belly. Place it on a plate, skin-side up, and season it with the regular table salt. Then, leave it uncovered in the fridge overnight.

2   The next day, get the meat out of the fridge and leave it to come up to room temperature (at least 30 minutes).

3   While the meat is coming up to room temperature, make the filling. Heat a frying pan over a medium heat, add the fennel seeds and chilli flakes and toast until you can smell them getting aromatic (about 30–40 seconds). Then, get them into a pestle and mortar with the garlic, fresh herbs, lemon zest and olive oil, mash them together until they form a paste of sorts. Add the flaky salt and season with black pepper.

4   Turn your pork belly upside down so that the meat is uppermost, then, using a sharp knife, make a diamond criss-cross pattern in the meat and begin to rub in the herby paste, completely covering the meat in an even layer.

5   Place 3–5 pieces of butcher's twine (long enough to tie around your meat) underneath the pork belly, equally spaced apart, then begin to roll the pork belly so that the skin is on the outside and the filling is encased. Using the middle string first, tie the pork belly in place with a simple double knot. (You can search 'butcher's knot' online to learn how to do it professionally, but anything that holds will do.)

6   Heat the air fryer to 120°C/250°F.

7   Rub the baking powder all over the skin of the rolled pork belly and spray the air-fryer basket and pork belly with some oil.

8   Place the porchetta in the air-fryer basket and cook for 25 minutes, then turn the air fryer up to 200°C/400°F and cook for a further 20 minutes, until it's cooked through. After this, if your skin still needs a bit more crisping to your liking, cook in 5-minute intervals until you get it just right.

Serves 4–6

800g–1kg/1¾–2¼lb piece of whole, bone-out pork belly, preferably a long piece (your butcher might be best for this)
1 tablespoon fennel seeds
1 tablespoon chilli flakes
3 garlic cloves
3 rosemary sprigs, leaves picked
3 thyme sprigs, leaves picked
1 lemon, zested
1 tablespoon olive oil
1 teaspoon sea-salt flakes
1 teaspoon baking powder
vegetable oil, for spraying
salt and ground black pepper

You will also need
butcher's twine (meat string)

MY SUGGESTIONS

You can easily replace the flavours in this recipe with any others you prefer. Black garlic is a delicious replacement for standard garlic; or you could even use smoked garlic. Alternatively, you could change up the herbs: try using lemon thyme or sage.

Pork is SOOO good with peppers, so serve this with the classic Italian peperonata, broccoli (see page 140) and some crispy cubes of potato (see page 120). YUM. For the peperonata, take 1 thinly sliced large onion, 6 deseeded and sliced peppers (red, orange and yellow ones), 3 crushed garlic cloves, 1 tablespoon of red wine vinegar (and more to taste), 1 tablespoon of tomato purée/paste and salt and pepper. Put a deep frying pan on a low-medium heat, add a large glug of olive oil, then add the onion and peppers and cook for 20 minutes, until soft. Add the garlic, vinegar and tomato purée/paste and season well. Leave to cook for a further 30 minutes – there should be no caramelisation, just soft, sticky peppers. Taste and adjust the seasoning to your liking.

For a more classic British approach, serve the porchetta with sautéed, buttered leeks, roast potatoes (see page 119), onion gravy (see page 46) and a dollop of apple sauce.

PORK CHOPS

I once cooked a pork chop in a job interview and it must've been nice as I was offered the job. This is just an anecdote, not a suggestion for next time you're in an interview, as I cannot guarantee Karen from HR will accept an air-fryer pork chop as an acceptable job application.

1   Season the pork chops liberally and rub them with olive oil. If you want to add any dry rubs or marinades (see notes below), do that now too.

2   Heat the air fryer to 180°C/350°F. Place the pork chops in the air-fryer basket and cook for 5–8 minutes, until just cooked. Cover and leave to rest for 10 minutes before serving.

Serves 4

4 pork chops
2 tablespoons olive oil
salt

MY SUGGESTIONS

Plate these up with mashed potatoes (see page 83), broccoli (see page 140) and a simple mustard sauce.

Try marinating these in pineapple and chilli. In a bowl, mix a mugful of pineapple juice, 1 finely grated garlic clove, 1 teaspoon of chilli flakes, 2 teaspoons of light soy sauce and 1 teaspoon of finely grated fresh ginger. Add the pork chops to the mixture, turn to coat and leave to marinate in the fridge for at least 30 minutes before you cook them as in the recipe.

Or, try an orange and mustard marinade. Simply mix together 2 tablespoons of wholegrain mustard, the zest and juice of 1 large orange, 1 teaspoon of runny honey, 1 tablespoon of thyme leaves and 3 tablespoons of light olive oil. Again, leave to marinate for at least 30 minutes (ideally longer) and then cook according to the recipe.

BBQ PORK RIBS

I'm never one to shy away from messy food, and BBQ ribs perfectly mess up one's face in just the right kind of way. You could always attempt to eat these with a knife and fork, but you'll be able to find me and a face-full of rib in the corner.

1   Heat the air fryer to 190°C/375°F.

2   Make a dry rub by mixing the paprika, garlic powder, onion powder, sugar and cayenne together in a bowl, and seasoning with salt and black pepper.

3   Get your pork ribs and rub this mixture all over. If you need to, cut your ribs into 2 or 3 chunks to help them fit into your air-fryer basket.

4   Spray the basket with oil, add the ribs and cook for 10 minutes. Then, slather the ribs in most of the barbecue sauce, flip them over and cook for a further 10 minutes. Add a final light glaze with barbecue sauce, then cook for a further 5–10 minutes, until piping hot and cooked through, with a sticky glaze.

MY SUGGESTIONS

Of course, you can change this up by using different sauces like sriracha, buffalo, honey soy glaze, the bourbon whiskey glaze from the burger recipe (would highly recommend checking that out; see page 68) and many other sauces to explore the world of ribs.

You can't go wrong with these ribs alongside your air-fryer corn-on-the-cob (see page 132), chips (see page 113) and coleslaw. To make your own quick and fresh coleslaw, just thinly slice half a red cabbage and 1 small red onion, and grate 2 carrots. Mix together with a teaspoon of sea-salt flakes and leave for 5 minutes, before draining off and adding 2 tablespoons of mayonnaise. Sometimes I even add a bit of grated apple or pear for a nice, sweet kick.

Serves 4

1 teaspoon smoked paprika
1 teaspoon garlic powder
1 teaspoon onion powder
1 tablespoon dark brown soft sugar
½ teaspoon cayenne pepper
1 rack of pork ribs (about 1kg/2¼lb in total)
olive oil, for spraying
100ml/7 tablespoons shop-bought barbecue sauce (I know it's cheating, but this is quick and easy)
salt and ground black pepper

PORK BELLY

Is there anything better in this world than a bit of perfectly crispy pork belly? It crisps up beautifully in the air fryer and you will all be fighting over who gets those crunchy bits of fat.

1   First, season the meat with salt and ground pepper and pat the skin dry with kitchen paper. Leave uncovered, skin-side up, in the fridge overnight. This will dry out the skin, which is key for a good crackle.

2   When you're ready to cook, bring the pork belly up to room temperature and score the skin diagonally, using a sharp knife.

3   Heat the air fryer to 220°C/425°F (or your air fryer's maximum temperature).

4   Toast the fennel seeds and peppercorns in a small frying pan over a medium heat, for 30 seconds, until fragrant. Tip the seeds and peppercorns into a mortar and crush with a pestle, then mix in the salt. Rub the mixture into the skin of the pork, making sure you get into all the nooks and crannies.

5   Place the pork belly in the air-fryer basket, skin-side up, and cook for 25–30 minutes, until the skin is starting to blister. Turn the temperature down to 160°C/325°F and cook for a further 1–1½ hours, until the meat easily pulls away from the bones and the skin is gloriously crackled and golden.

MY SUGGESTIONS

Serve this up hot in a bread bap, with apple sauce and stuffing, and some gravy to pour all over. It's a classic but it gets a crowd fed. Or serve as a roast dinner, plated with new or hasselback potatoes (see page 114), mixed vegetables, cauliflower cheese (see page 157) and gravy.

Or, try it with bao buns! Oh, it's just the best. Glaze your crispy pork belly in char siu sauce, which you can get from Asian supermarkets. Steam or microwave your bao buns (again, get them in the freezer aisle in Asian supermarkets), add some pickled radish, kewpie mayonnaise and crispy onion along with the pork. It's a meal made in heaven.

Serves 4–6

1kg/2¼lb piece of bone-in pork belly
2 teaspoons fennel seeds
1 teaspoon black peppercorns, plus ground pepper to season
1 teaspoon sea-salt flakes, plus extra to season

HOMEMADE SCOTCH EGG

This is a throwback to one of the first dishes I made in my first ever kitchen job. Shout-out to the Scotch eggs of The Queen's Head Inn, Bromsgrove, that I'd make time and time again back in 2011. I wish we'd had an air fryer to speed up the process for equally delicious results.

1 Heat the air fryer to 130°C/270°F.

2 Put the 4 whole eggs in the air-fryer basket and cook them for 9 minutes, which will be just enough to soft-boil them. Meanwhile, prepare a bowl of ice-cold water.

3 Once the time is up, transfer the eggs to the icy water and leave to cool (about 5 minutes). Once cool, peel them and set aside.

4 In a bowl, mix the sausagemeat, dried herbs and garlic powder with your hands until it forms a paste-like consistency. Season with salt and pepper.

5 Using kitchen paper, dry the peeled eggs.

6 Gather three bowls. Season the flour and tip that into one bowl. Add the beaten eggs to the second, and the breadcrumbs to the third.

7 Using one quarter of the sausagemeat mixture, mould the meat around one of the boiled eggs as evenly as possible, aiming for the same thickness all the way around. Repeat so that all the eggs are covered in sausagemeat.

8 Heat the air fryer to 180°C/350°F.

9 One by one, dip the wrapped eggs first in flour (dusting off any excess), then in the beaten egg and finally in the breadcrumbs to coat fully.

10 Put the eggs into the air-fryer basket and cook for 12 minutes, until the sausage is cooked through and the coating is golden.

Makes 4

4 whole eggs, plus
  2 extra, beaten
500g/about 1lb
  sausagemeat
½ teaspoon dried mixed
  herbs
½ teaspoon garlic
  powder
2 tablespoons plain/all
  purpose flour
200g/4 cups Panko
  breadcrumbs
salt and ground black
  pepper

MY SUGGESTIONS

Try using different meat minces to make the coating; or if you're wanting veggie, use a meat alternative.

Best way to serve? Hot and straight out of the air fryer with some piccalilli and a bag of crisps – just like being at the gastro pub.

TOAD IN THE HOLE

I have to admit, I've never been that good at making Yorkshire puddings so I had to ask my mom for this recipe. She is a very talented cook and her Yorkshires are always big, puffy and crispy so this is really 'Vicky's toad in the hole'. Thanks Mom. No matter how old you are, you always end up needing your mom!

1 Make your pudding batter by simply whisking the milk, flour and eggs together and then get the mix into a jug and in the fridge for at least 1 hour to rest.

2 Find a baking tray, or metal tray that fits in your air fryer (you may have to do two trays to use up all the mixture – but it's a quick dish, so no problem).

3 Meanwhile, heat the air fryer to 200°C/400°F.

4 Once the batter has had time to rest, get all the sausages (or half if you're doing it in two batches) and 2 tablespoons of oil into the tray and cook for 7 minutes.

5 While everything is still super-hot and in the air fryer, pour in the batter, to come halfway up the sausages (or however much fits best in your tray).

6 Cook for a further 8–10 minutes, until the Yorkshire pudding has risen in all its glory. Remove from the air fryer and serve.

MY SUGGESTIONS

You can add herbs and spices to the Yorkshire batter: chopped thyme, rosemary or sage would be good. You could incorporate a little stuffing ball into your toad in the hole, if you like.

Serve this with green veggies, a red wine gravy and sweet potato cubes (see page 126).

Serves 4

100ml/7 tablespoons whole milk
110g/scant 1 cup plain/all purpose flour
4 eggs
2–4 tablespoons vegetable oil
8 pork sausages (I like chipolatas, but it's totally up to you)

LAMB CHOPS

You'll soon find out I am a mint sauce FIEND. Lather it all over those chops, bathe in it after and you've got yourself the perfect evening. Honestly, I love mint sauce so much. Then again, having read all the intros of this book again, it sounds like I'm a fiend to pretty much every type of food and that's no lie. Except for jelly. Never jelly ... actually don't they call mint sauce mint jelly in the USA? Now I'm confused.

1 Heat the air fryer to 180°C/350°F. Season the lamb generously with salt and pepper.

2 Set a frying pan over a medium heat, add the chops to the pan, skin-side down, and render the fat, until it goes golden. Drain the fat from the pan and sear the lamb for a minute on each side.

3 Place the lamb in the air-fryer basket and cook for 8–10 minutes, until cooked but still pink in the middle. Rest for 5 minutes before serving.

Serves 4

4 Barnsley chops or 8 lamb loin chops
salt and ground black pepper

MY SUGGESTIONS

If you can't find Barnsley chops then use 8 loin chops and cook for 5 minutes less.

Before cooking, try coating the lamb with a spiced yogurt marinade. Simply mix 3 tablespoons of Greek yogurt with 2 tablespoons of tandoori spice mix, the juice of half a lemon and 1 teaspoon of cooking oil. Leave to marinate for a minimum of 30 minutes and then cook as per the recipe.

Or, try a garlic and rosemary marinade. In a bowl, mix 3 crushed garlic cloves, the chopped leaves of 4 rosemary sprigs, the zest of 1 lemon, 1 tablespoon of olive oil and salt and pepper. Simply cover the lamb in the marinade and leave for a minimum of 30 minutes. Cook according to the recipe.

I think the best way to serve a lamb chop is with lashings of mint sauce, and with peas, roast potatoes (see page 119) and gravy. Nothing compares and it takes me back home. But, if you want something spicy, why not try with red lentil dhal and a coriander/cilantro dressing? Or with sweet potato cubes (see page 126), mixed veg and a mint salad dressing.

ROAST LAMB

You know it's spring when you can smell the lamb in the oven, so now smell its deliciousness radiating from the air fryer instead. Get plenty of mint sauce on the side – and when I say plenty, I'd have it swimming in it. Delicious.

1   Make a marinade. Mix together the olive oil, thyme leaves, garlic, lemon zest and juice, Aleppo pepper, salt and a generous amount of black pepper.

2   Using a sharp knife, make several slashes in the skin of the lamb shoulder and pour over the marinade. Cover the meat and leave it in the fridge for at least 2 hours, or overnight if you can.

3   About an hour before you are ready to cook, take the lamb out of the fridge and bring it up to room temperature.

4   Heat the air fryer to 220°C/425°F (or your air fryer's maximum temperature).

5   Place the lamb in a baking tray that will fit in the air fryer or use foil to encase the lamb, just don't fully close it yet. Leave the foil open and cook for 30 minutes, until crisp.

6   Reduce the temperature to 140°C/285°F. Add a cupful of water to the baking tray or your foil parcel. If using a baking tray, cover tightly with foil, and if you are making it wrapped in foil, then close up the opening so the lamb is fully encased. Cook for 3–4 hours, until the meat easily pulls away from the bone. Check the lamb a couple of times, adding more water if needed. Leave the lamb to rest for at least 20 minutes before serving.

Serves 4

100ml/7 tablespoons olive oil
8 thyme sprigs, leaves picked
6 garlic cloves, crushed
1 lemon, zested and juiced
2 teaspoons Aleppo pepper
2 teaspoons salt
1.4kg/about 3lb bone-in lamb shoulder
ground black pepper

MY SUGGESTIONS

A large joint of meat like a lamb shoulder doesn't have to be served only as a roast dinner on a Sunday afternoon. It can be an easy way to feed a crowd on a weekday. I like to serve this with the rice-stuffed peppers (see page 147) and roast Med veg (see page 153) and use any juices from the lamb as the sauce.

If you are having it as a roast dinner, use up leftovers by making little lamb tacos with corn tortillas, lime pickled onions, crumbled feta, mint sauce and salad. It's the perfect way to use the same dish but with completely different flavours so you don't get bored.

LAMB KOFTA

Koftas have become one of my go-to dinners as they make the perfect meal wrapped in a pitta, topped with any of your favourite combinations of mint yogurt, pickled onions, chillies and anything else your heart desires. They are always a crowd-pleaser and, thanks to the air fryer, can be an even simpler and quicker meal to make for the whole family. Serve all the elements on the table and just let everyone go mad assembling the wraps themselves. My kinda dinner.

Makes 10

½ teaspoon fennel seeds
½ teaspoon black peppercorns
½ teaspoon coriander seeds
500g/about 1lb lamb mince/ground lamb
¼ teaspoon ground cinnamon
½ teaspoon cayenne pepper
1 garlic clove, crushed
1 teaspoon sea-salt flakes
olive oil, for brushing
ground black pepper

1   Warm a small frying pan over a medium heat. Add the fennel seeds, black peppercorns and coriander seeds and toast for 30 seconds, until fragrant. Tip into a mortar and crush with a pestle. Set aside.

2   Get your lamb mince into a bowl and add the crushed toasted spices, along with the cinnamon, cayenne pepper, crushed garlic and sea salt. Season generously with pepper, then get stuck in and mix together thoroughly using your hands. Leave to marinate in the fridge for at least 1 hour, or overnight if you can.

3   About 1 hour before you're ready to cook, remove the lamb mixture from the fridge and bring it up to room temperature.

4   Heat the air fryer to 200°C/400°F.

5   Roll the lamb mixture into balls, each about the size of a golf ball. Shape the balls into elongated ovals (like a squashed rugby ball), if you like – or leave them as balls. You should end up with 10 kofta.

6   Brush the kofta all over with a little olive oil and put them in the air-fryer basket, making sure there is plenty of space between them (do this in batches, depending on the size of your air fryer).

7   Cook for 9–10 minutes, turning halfway through, until cooked through and golden. Set aside to rest for a few minutes before serving.

MY SUGGESTIONS

This dish is perfect with some tahini yogurt (simply mix together 3 tablespoons of Greek yogurt, 2 tablespoons of tahini, the juice of half a lemon and a pinch of salt, then add just enough water to thin the sauce) and some quick pickled onions (just slice up 2–3 small red onions and get them in a bowl. Cover with boiling water for a few seconds, then drain and squeeze over the juice of a lime and a sprinkle of salt and let them sit for a 30 minutes – the easiest pickles you'll ever make). You'll also need some flatbreads or pittas, some salad leaves and chips.

BEEF AND PORK MEATBALLS

Get your balls in the air fryer and put this top of your list for dinner this week. I don't think you can go wrong with meatballs.

1   Tip the bread into a large mixing bowl and cover with milk. Set aside for about 20 minutes, then mash with a fork and pour away any excess liquid.

2   Meanwhile, toast the fennel seeds in a frying pan over a medium heat for 30 seconds, until fragrant. Set aside.

3   Add the pork, beef, egg, garlic, parsley and fennel seeds to the soaked bread, and season generously with salt and pepper. Mix together, using your hands, until evenly combined.

4   Roll the mixture into neat balls, each about the size of a ping-pong ball, then let the balls rest for at least 30 minutes before cooking. (You can prepare the balls up to a day in advance – just remember to bring them up to room temperature again before you cook.)

5   Heat the air fryer to 200°C/400°F. Lightly drizzle the balls with olive oil and roll them around in it until they are evenly coated.

6   Place the meatballs in the air-fryer basket, ensuring that there is plenty of space around each (you might have to do this in batches, depending on the size of your air fryer). Cook for 10–12 minutes, turning halfway through, until cooked through.

Makes 24

75g/2 medium slices day-old bread, crusts removed and torn into small pieces
whole milk, to cover the bread
1 teaspoon fennel seeds
250g/9oz pork mince/ ground pork
250g/9oz beef mince/ ground beef
1 egg
1 garlic clove, crushed
a small handful of flat-leaf parsley, finely chopped
olive oil, for drizzling
salt and ground black pepper

MY SUGGESTIONS

The classic way to serve meatballs is with pasta in a tomato sauce. For a simple tomato sauce take 700g/1½lb of chopped fresh tomatoes (any kind), 3 sliced garlic cloves, half a bunch of basil leaves and good olive oil, as well as salt and pepper, a bit of sugar and vinegar for seasoning. Get a saucepan nice and hot, add a good layer of oil to the pan and then half of the tomatoes, and cook until juicy. Then add the garlic and season well. After a couple of minutes, add the rest of the tomatoes and cook for a further 5–10 minutes, until everything is cooked down and saucy. Tear in the basil leaves, taste and season with a sprinkling of sugar and vinegar if it needs it.

Alternatively, try a meatball sub. Layer 4 sub rolls with warm tomato sauce (as above), meatballs, a few slices of mozzarella and get these into the air fryer for another 5 minutes, until all melted and toasted. Sprinkle with basil leaves to serve.

BEEF BURGERS

I love a burger, and layering them up is my favourite part. There's so much in this book that could go in that bun – I'd go for the mozzarella dippers (see page 167) or onion rings (see page 156) and hash browns (see page 125) on top of these delicious burgers.

1   Warm 2 tablespoons of the olive oil in a saucepan over a medium heat. Add the onion and cook for about 10 minutes, until softened and gently golden.

2   Tip your cooked onion into a mixing bowl, along with the beef, egg, breadcrumbs, Worcestershire sauce, Parmesan, salt and a good amount of black pepper. Shape the mix into 6 equal-sized burgers, cover and leave them in the fridge for at least 30 minutes.

3   Remove the burgers from the fridge and bring them up to room temperature before you cook (this can take up to an hour).

4   Heat the air fryer to 200°C/400°F.

5   Rub the remaining oil over the burgers, place them in the air-fryer basket and cook for 10–12 minutes, until crisp on the outside and cooked through (you may need to do this in batches).

MY SUGGESTIONS

To recreate the American classic, you'll need a toasted sesame bun, some lettuce, a couple of slices each of onion and tomato, the burger and some American cheese, mayo, ketchup and pickles.

Or try a FULLY LOADED, fully stacked, fully flavoured burger. You will need: 2 rashers of crispy, streaky bacon per person, 1 hash brown per person (see page 125), 1 onion ring per person (see page 156), some salad if you want it, a burger with a slice of smoked cheese melted on it and some Bourbon whiskey sticky sauce. To make the sauce, gently fry 150g/1 heaping cup of shallots in a saucepan on a medium heat. Once translucent, add the grated cloves of half a garlic bulb (yes, bulb) and 1cm/½-inch piece of fresh ginger, grated, and cook for 3 minutes until aromatic. Add 50ml/3 tablespoons of Bourbon whiskey and simmer for 2 minutes. Add 95ml/7 tablespoons of sweet teriyaki sauce, 2 tablespoons of tomato chutney, 100g/½ cup of dark muscovado sugar, a 227g/8.25oz tin of pineapple rings (fruit finely chopped and syrup included), 3 tablespoons of maple syrup, 1 teaspoon of cider vinegar and 100–200ml/7 tablespoons-generous ¾ cup of water to the pan. Simmer for 1 hour until you get a thick glaze consistency.

Serves 6

3 tablespoons olive oil
1 onion, finely chopped
500g/about 1lb beef mince/ground beef
1 egg
50g/½ cup dried breadcrumbs
a splash of Worcestershire sauce
30g/⅓ cup Parmesan, grated
½ teaspoon salt
ground black pepper

CRISPY SHREDDED BEEF

My order of choice from my local takeaway, and I'm always down for a fakeaway recipe to recreate the deliciousness at home. Serve with noodles, rice, or even salad for health if you fancy it.

1 Get your beef in a bowl with the soy sauce, sesame oil and white pepper. Turn the meat to coat in the marinade and set it aside for 10 minutes (this is a good time to prepare the veggies for the sauce, if you haven't already).

2 Heat the air fryer to 220°C/425°F (or your air fryer's maximum temperature).

3 Toss the beef in the cornflour and place it in the air-fryer basket, making sure there is space between each piece. Cook for 3–4 minutes, until crisp, then remove the beef pieces from the fryer and sit them on a plate. (You might have to do this in batches, depending on the size of your air fryer.)

4 While the beef is cooking, start the sauce. Warm the sesame oil in a wok or large frying pan over a high heat. Add the onions and cook for 2–3 minutes, then add the spring onions, garlic, peppers and ginger and cook for another 3–4 minutes, until everything is tender. Add the soy sauce, rice wine vinegar, sriracha, sugar and ½ cup of water and bubble briskly until reduced to a sticky glaze consistency. Taste to check the seasoning and adjust with the vinegar, sugar, soy or sriracha as necessary – it should be a balance of sweet, salty and sour.

5 By now the beef should be ready. Briefly toss the crispy beef through the vegetable sauce and serve straight away.

MY SUGGESTIONS

This beef goes so well with a sticky rice, sliced spring onion and fresh chilli. Simple but effective. Add a crispy fried egg for extra luxury.

Or, try serving it with vermicelli rice noodles, sugar snap peas and thin slices of cooked carrot. All tossed with the sauce and sprinkled with spring onion and sliced chilli.

Serves 4

500g/about 1lb beef rump or sirloin, cut into thin strips (about 1.5cm/½-inch wide)
2 tablespoons dark soy sauce
2 tablespoons sesame oil
¼ teaspoon ground white pepper
2 tablespoons cornflour/ cornstarch

For the sauce
2 tablespoons sesame oil
2 onions, finely sliced
3 spring onions, finely sliced
2 garlic cloves, finely sliced
2 red peppers, deseeded and finely sliced
30g/2-inch piece fresh ginger, peeled and cut into matchsticks
2 tablespoons dark soy sauce
4 tablespoons rice wine vinegar
4 tablespoons sriracha
2 tablespoons light brown soft sugar

THE CLASSIC ROAST BEEF

Your Sunday dinners just got easier, and the answer is your air fryer. Throw your beef into the tray and it'll cook as beautifully as your normal roast. You can't go wrong with this classic.

1 An hour before you're ready to cook, bring the beef up to room temperature.

2 Heat the air fryer to 220°C/425°F (or your air fryer's maximum temperature).

3 Pat the beef dry with kitchen paper and season generously with salt and pepper. Drizzle the beef with oil and rub it in using your hands.

4 Place the beef in the air-fryer basket and cook for 15 minutes, then reduce the temperature to 100°C/210°F and cook for a further 40–45 minutes to give a rare joint (a meat thermometer, if you have one, should read 52°C/126°F). Remove the beef from the basket, cover it and rest it for at least 20 minutes before serving.

MY SUGGESTIONS

Try rubbing the beef with a spice mix before you cook it. Here are a couple of spicy suggestions:

Smoky bbq: Mix together 1–2 teaspoons of cayenne pepper with 1 teaspoon each of chilli flakes, smoked paprika, garlic powder, onion powder, ground cumin, ground coriander, salt and ground black pepper. Just rub it all over the meat and cook.

Classic: Mix together 1 teaspoon each of salt, ground black pepper, onion powder, garlic powder and dried thyme. Rub it on the meat before cooking.

Serves 4–6

1.25kg/2¾lb beef roasting joint
vegetable oil
salt and ground black pepper

FISH

HONEY SOY SALMON

Beautifully flaky salmon seasoned perfectly with a sweet, sticky, salty glaze. Salmon is easily one of my favourite fish and it's so simple to cook with great results in the air fryer.

1   Make a marinade by whisking together your soy sauce, honey, sesame oil, garlic, ginger and chilli flakes. Pour the marinade over the salmon and set aside in the fridge for at least 30 minutes.

2   Heat the air fryer to 180°C/350°F.

3   Lift the salmon fillets out of the marinade (reserve the marinade in the bowl), place them in the air-fryer basket and cook for 7–9 minutes, until cooked and flaky.

4   Meanwhile, tip the reserved marinade into a small saucepan over a medium heat, add ½ cup of water and reduce until glossy. Taste to check the seasoning – you might need to add a splash of rice wine vinegar and honey to balance the flavours. Blitz until smooth if you like.

5   Serve the salmon with the sauce drizzled over.

MY SUGGESTIONS

Try this salmon served with steamed rice, grilled spring onions (see page 131) or broccoli (see page 140), crispy shallots (the ones from the supermarket) some pickled veg, or with soba noodles and longstem broccoli/broccolini. Or use roasted sweet potatoes as the base with any veg you fancy.

Serves 4

3 tablespoons dark soy sauce
3 tablespoons runny honey
1 tablespoon sesame oil
2 garlic cloves, crushed
4cm/1½-inch piece fresh ginger, finely chopped or grated (no need to peel)
1 teaspoon chilli flakes
4 skinless salmon fillets

SALMON EN CROUTE

Salmon wrapped up in a lovely bit of pastry – you can't go wrong. Yes, we love a bit of fast food, and yes, a takeaway is nice every so often, but a homely plate of salmon en croute with asparagus? I'm instantly taken home with my nan, having a lovely ol' time.

1 Set a large frying pan over a medium heat, add the watercress and cook for 3–5 minutes, until any water has been released and evaporated. Once cool enough to handle, squeeze out any excess water, roughly chop and add it to a mixing bowl. Add the parsley, crème fraîche, lemon zest and egg yolk to the bowl, stir to combine and season generously.

2 Unroll the puff pastry sheets and place one of them on a piece of greaseproof paper.

3 Trim the salmon to fit onto one puff pastry sheet and pat it dry with kitchen paper. Lightly season it with salt and pepper, then smear the top with Dijon mustard. Sit the salmon in the middle of the pastry and spread the watercress mix across the top. Top with the second sheet of pastry. Using your hands, smooth out any air bubbles and crimp the edges, sealing it all up. Chill in the fridge for at least 30 minutes.

4 Heat the air fryer to 200°C/400°F. Take the salmon parcel out of the fridge and brush the pastry with the beaten egg. Use a knife to make a small incision in the top.

5 Using the greaseproof paper, lift the salmon into the air-fryer basket and bake for 20–25 minutes, until golden. Leave to stand for 10 minutes before slicing and serving.

Serves 4

160g/6oz watercress
30g/heaping ½ cup flat-leaf parsley, leaves finely chopped
4 tablespoons crème fraîche
1 lemon, zested
1 egg yolk, plus 1 lightly beaten egg to glaze
1 side of skinless salmon fillet (about 800g/1¾lb)
2–3 tablespoons Dijon mustard
2 sheets of ready-made puff pastry
salt and ground black pepper

MY SUGGESTIONS

Keep it classic with this dish. I serve it with a green salad or air-fryer asparagus (see page 131), herb butter and a glass of cold champagne. Why not? If you're whipping this up, it's a special occasion.

A side of pickled cucumber is also a classic serving. To make a quick pickle, cut a cucumber in half lengthways, use a teaspoon to scoop out and discard the seeds. Thinly slice the cucumber and place it in a colander. Sprinkle with 1 teaspoon of sea-salt flakes and leave for 10 minutes, then squeeze dry. In a saucepan add 50ml/3 tablespoons of white wine vinegar, 2 tablespoons of white sugar and 1 tablespoon of water and heat until the sugar has dissolved. Once cooled, add in the cucumber and leave for a further 20–30 minutes before eating.

HADDOCK AND PARSLEY SAUCE

A simple dinner that always reminds me of my mom when it's served up with some delicious mashed potato (see page 83). A fresh, classic dish that shines in the air fryer.

1   First, make your parsley sauce. Melt the butter in a small saucepan over a low-medium heat. Add the flour and cook for 4-5 minutes, stirring almost continuously, then gradually beat in the milk, little by little, until you have a smooth sauce.

2   Add the parsley, then add the cream and season generously with salt and pepper. Simmer until the sauce has thickened (about 5 minutes). Remove the sauce from the heat and set aside.

3   Heat the air fryer to 180°C/350°F.

4   Pat the fish dry with kitchen paper, season lightly with salt and pepper and drizzle with olive oil.

5   Place the fillets in the air-fryer basket, making sure there is plenty of space between each piece, and cook for 9-10 minutes, until just cooked through.

6   Gently warm the parsley sauce and pour it over the fish to serve.

MY SUGGESTIONS

You could season the haddock with roasted ground cumin for a more in-depth roasted flavour that goes so well with the parsley sauce.

This dish is perfect served with crushed buttered new potatoes and seasonal vegetables.

Serves 4

30g/2 tablespoons butter
30g/¼ cup plain/all purpose flour
500ml/2 cups whole milk
30g/heaping ½ cup flat-leaf parsley, leaves and stems finely chopped
200ml/generous ¾ cup double/heavy cream
4 skin-on, pin-boned haddock fillets (about 140g/5oz each)
olive oil, for drizzling
salt and ground black pepper

SMOKED HADDOCK EN PAPILLOTE

Such a posh way to say cooked in a paper bag! This method of cooking is ideal for low-hassle deliciousness. Using greaseproof paper to make a little steam oven surrounding your smoked haddock just ensures you get perfectly cooked fish that's filled with flavour. And it looks very fancy on the dinner table.

1 Heat the air fryer to 180°C/350°F.

2 Pat the fish dry with kitchen paper and season.

3 Sit a piece of haddock in the middle of a sheet of greaseproof paper, add one of the pieces of butter, a handful of parsley, 1 bay leaf, a splash of wine (if using) and a good grind of black pepper. Bring the sides of the paper up over the fish and scrunch tightly to seal. Repeat with the remaining ingredients, each with their own greaseproof paper parcel.

4 Place the parcels in the air-fryer basket and cook for 8–10 minutes, until just cooked. Leave to stand for 5 minutes before serving.

MY SUGGESTIONS

This dish is delicious with mashed potatoes. To make my perfect mash, peel 6 Maris Piper or Russet potatoes and slice into 2cm rounds, get them into a pan and cover with cold water. Add 1 tablespoon of salt to the pan and bring to the boil on a high heat. Boil for 10–15 minutes, or until the potatoes are soft and fall off the end of a knife when poked. Drain the spuds, leave them in the colander, place a tea towel over the top and leave for 5–10 minutes. Then push the potatoes though a sieve to give super smooth mash. Add 50–75g of butter and mix well.

I also suggest warm crusty bread and brown butter caper dressing to go with this dish. Get 80g/5 tablespoons of butter in a pan and cook on a medium heat until it's frothy and smells nutty. Then add 1 tablespoon of capers (chopped), 1 handful of flat-leaf parsley (chopped) and a squeeze of lemon. Give it a stir and serve it over the fish.

Serves 4

4 skin-on, pin-boned smoked haddock fillets (about 140g/ 5oz each)
60g/4 tablespoons butter, divided into 4 equal pieces
30g/⅔ cup flat-leaf parsley, leaves and stems roughly chopped
4 bay leaves
small glass of white wine (optional)
salt and ground black pepper

WHOLE BASS

Those who get eating a whole fish get it. It's 10,000% a bit of me. I love picking the meat from the bone, feeling a bit Neanderthal (good word) as I get to the extra-good bits. Leave me alone with a whole fish and I'll be busy in heaven for hours.

1 Heat the air fryer to 180°C/350°F.

2 Season the sea bass generously and drizzle them with the olive oil. Use a sharp knife to make 3 diagonal cuts in each fish.

3 Place the fish in the air-fryer basket and cook for 12–15 minutes, until just cooked through.

MY SUGGESTIONS

You can serve this supper easily on a bed of mixed leaves like rocket, watercress, lamb's lettuce and some mixed herbs, and then on the side have some thyme and garlic potato wedges and pair with a lemon butter (melt some butter and add the zest and juice of 1 lemon, a grated garlic clove and a bunch of flat-leaf parsley, chopped).

Alternatively, serve it up with some pan-roasted, butter-soaked sliced fennel with a squeeze of lemon.

You could also add slices of lemon to the cavity of the bass and this will add flavour throughout the fish.

Serves 4

2 whole sea bass (about 300g/10oz each, or as large as will fit in your fryer)
2–3 tablespoons olive oil
salt and ground black pepper

MISO-GLAZED COD

The cod shines in this beautiful fish dish with its Asian-inspired glaze. Miso is a salty, fermented soybean paste that add loads of umami flavour to balance the dish perfectly. (Oh, that sounded so cheffy!)

1 Put all the ingredients except the cod in a small saucepan over a high heat. Bring to the boil, and boil until the sugar has melted and the miso has dissolved. Transfer the mixture to a jug and leave it, uncovered, in the fridge to cool.

2 Once the marinade is cold, get your cod fillets in a bowl and pour the marinade over them. Turn the fillets to coat, then cover the bowl and put it in the fridge. Leave the fillets to marinate for at least 3 hours, but preferably overnight. Remove the bowl from the fridge to let the cod come up to room temperature for 20 minutes before you start cooking.

3 Heat the air fryer to 180°C/350°F.

4 Remove the cod from the marinade (reserve the marinade in the bowl), spray the air-fryer basket with oil and place the fillets inside, spacing them apart if there's room (but it's not essential in this case). Cook for 10–12 minutes, brushing a little of the leftover marinade over the cod about halfway through the cooking time to give an extra glaze, until the cod is brown on the outside and flaking apart.

MY SUGGESTIONS

This miso cod can be served with an array of sides, but I like it with boiled brown rice, covered in miso glaze from the cod, fresh green veg and a cucumber pickle (see page 79).

You could also serve this like a donburi or poke bowl, with white rice, soft air-fryer boiled egg soaked in soy sauce (see page 144), thinly sliced mangetout, matchstick spring onions, shredded crispy seaweed, pickled radish, edamame beans, sesame seeds and chilli. Then in the bowl you arrange all those ingredients in sections, so it's like a rainbow bowl topped with the miso cod. Such a filling but light meal, which is full of flavour and nutrients.

Serves 4

4 tablespoons white miso
4 tablespoons mirin
3 tablespoons rice wine (sake)
3 tablespoons dark soy sauce
3 tablespoons granulated sugar
2 garlic cloves, bashed
small knob/½-inch piece of fresh ginger, sliced (no need to peel)
4 skin-on, boneless cod loin fillets (each about 140g/5oz; not the tail ends)
vegetable oil, for spraying

FISH CAKES

Ohhh who doesn't love a fish cake? The tasty, easy way to get fish into your diet. These full-of-flavour little fish-cake balls are ideal for using up anything left in the fridge too, which is always a bonus.

1   Boil the potatoes in salted water for 20–25 minutes, until completely soft. Drain and mash until smooth, adding the knob of butter as you go.

2   Meanwhile, add your fish to a large shallow pan, along with the milk, bay, parsley stalks and peppercorns. Cover with a lid and simmer very gently for 5–10 minutes, until just cooked. Carefully extract the fish and set it aside to cool.

3   Using your hands, carefully break the fish fillets into pieces and add the pieces to the mashed potato. Roughly chop the parsley leaves and add these too. Season generously and stir to combine, being careful not to break up the pieces of fish. Roll the mixture into 16 balls, each about the size of a golf ball, and chill them in the fridge for at least 30 minutes.

4   Heat the air fryer to 200°C/400°F.

5   Next, find three shallow bowls. Crack the eggs into one and whisk gently. Tip the flour into the second bowl and the breadcrumbs into the third. Lightly season the breadcrumbs.

6   Using one hand for the wet ingredients (eggs) and the other for the dry ingredients (flour and breadcrumbs), one by one dip the fish cakes in the flour, then the egg, then the breadcrumbs, coating each one, and place them on a lined baking tray.

7   Lightly spray the fish cakes with oil. Place in the air-fryer basket, leaving plenty of space between each one. Cook for 10–15 minutes, until golden.

MY SUGGESTIONS

There's so much you can change in these little fishy balls to make them truly your own. Change up the fish you use, or add spices or different herbs, or add cheese to the mash.

Serve with a sauce, such as tartar sauce, parsley sauce (see page 80), garlic mayo, lemon mayo, or perinaise or hot sauce. Some lemon wedges and a fresh side salad complete the look.

Serves 4

1kg/2¼lb Maris Piper, Russet or King Edward potatoes, peeled and cut into even-sized pieces
knob of butter
1kg/2¼lb white fish fillets, such as cod, haddock or pollock
1 litre/4 cups whole milk
2 bay leaves
30g/1oz flat-leaf parsley, leaves and stalks separated
8 black peppercorns
2 eggs
40g/⅓ cup plain/all purpose flour
100g/2 cups Panko breadcrumbs
olive oil, for spraying
salt and ground black pepper

BREADED COD

Mover over captain B******e, there's a new skipper in town ... healthier and tastier. Moist, flaky fish encased in crispy breadcrumbs. They can be served with anything you fancy – chips, new potatoes, rice, salad ... the list is endless and delicious.

1   Heat the air fryer to 220°C/425°F (or your air fryer's maximum temperature).

2   Pat the fish dry with kitchen paper and season the fillets all over.

3   Find three shallow bowls. Crack the eggs into one and whisk gently. Add the flour to the second bowl and the breadcrumbs to the third. Lightly season the breadcrumbs.

4   Using one hand for the wet ingredients (eggs) and the other for the dry ingredients (flour and breadcrumbs), dip a piece of fish in the flour, then the egg, followed by the breadcrumbs. Repeat the process for a second time to coat fully, and place it on a lined baking tray. Repeat with the remaining fish fillets.

5   Lightly spray the breaded fish with oil. Place the fish fillets in the air-fryer basket, leaving plenty of space between each one. Cook for 13–15 minutes, until golden.

Serves 4

4 cod fillets (about 140g/5oz each)
2 eggs
40g/⅓ cup plain/all purpose flour
100g/2 cups Panko breadcrumbs
olive oil, for spraying
salt and ground black pepper

MY SUGGESTIONS

Serve with wedges of lemon, and sriracha mayo, tartar sauce, smoky ketchup or aïoli. Swap for other firm, white fish, such as haddock, pollock or coley, if you like.

You can turn the breaded cod fillets into goujons if you prefer. Cut each fillet into strips, each about 3cm/1¼ inches wide and roughly the length of your index finger. Coat the goujons in the egg, flour and breadcrumbs, lay them on a lined baking tray, then lightly drizzle or spray them with olive oil. Place them in the air-fryer basket, leaving plenty of space between each piece, and cook for 6–7 minutes, until golden. If you're using freshly caught fish, leave it in the fridge for 1–3 days before using, as this will help each goujon to hold its shape. This is particularly important if you're using freshly caught pollock.

To make a classic fish finger butty, simply butter up some soft white bread, smother in tartar sauce and ketchup and add your freshly cooked goujons. Douse in malt vinegar and serve with mushy peas.

FISH KEBAB TACOS

A Mexican-inspired dinner that's fun to assemble at the table and just as fun to eat. Serve with your deliciously fresh pico de gallo to cut through on your hot, toasted tacos and the whole family will be having the best day ever.

1 To make the pico de gallo, simply mix your tomatoes, coriander stalks and leaves, onion and chilli together in a bowl. Add the lime juice to taste, along with the salt flakes and sugar. Taste to check the seasoning and adjust as necessary – it should be a balance of sweet, sharp, salty and sour. Set aside while you get everything else together.

2 To make the slaw, combine the slaw ingredients in a bowl, reserving a few of the coriander leaves to serve.

3 Heat the air fryer to 100°C/210°F.

4 Dry-fry the tortillas in batches in a hot frying pan until toasted. Keep each batch warm in the air fryer while you toast the remainder.

5 Place the goujons in the air-fryer basket, warming them for 3 minutes with the tortillas.

6 To serve, divide the slaw between the tortillas, top with a couple of pieces of fish, squeeze over some lime and top with a spoonful of pico de gallo. Scatter over the reserved coriander leaves to garnish.

MY SUGGESTIONS

Serve with some hot sauce, sliced avocado, some cheesy nachos, extra salsas, corn ribs (see page 135) and a few cold, cold beers. Or Fanta!

Serves 4

1 x fish goujons (see notes on page 91)
12–16 small corn tortillas
1–2 limes, cut into wedges

For the pico de gallo
3 plum tomatoes or 150g/1 cup cherry tomatoes, deseeded and finely chopped
15g/5 tablespoons coriander/cilantro, leaves roughly chopped and stalks finely chopped
½ red onion, very finely chopped
1–2 green chillies, deseeded and finely chopped
1–2 limes, juiced, to taste
big pinch of sea-salt flakes
pinch of sugar

For the slaw
¼ white cabbage, finely shredded
½ red onion, finely sliced
15g/5 tablespoons coriander/cilantro, leaves roughly chopped and stalks finely chopped

94

SCAMPI

When I was younger, I was a scampi girl. I would always get scampi from the chippy. But making them yourself and air-frying them is a much healthier and cheaper alternative. They are seafood nuggets that can be doused in salt and lemon juice and dipped into flavourful sauces.

1   Heat the air fryer to 220°C/425°F (or your air fryer's maximum temperature).

2   Find three shallow bowls. Crack the eggs into one bowl and whisk gently. Add the flour to the second bowl and the breadcrumbs to the third. Lightly season the breadcrumbs.

3   Using one hand for the wet ingredients (eggs) and the other for the dry ingredients (flour and breadcrumbs), dip a langoustine tail in the flour, then the egg, then the breadcrumbs. Repeat the process for a second time, to coat fully, and place the scampi on a lined baking tray. Repeat with the remaining ingredients.

4   Lightly spray the scampi with oil. Place them in the air-fryer basket, leaving plenty of space between each piece. Cook for 5–6 minutes, until golden. Scatter over some sea salt and ground black pepper to serve.

MY SUGGESTIONS

Sometimes simplicity is key, so I like to serve scampi with wedges of lemon, chips and aïoli. They are just so tasty, why would you want to mask that delicate flavour with much else? To be fair, a sweet chilli dip with them is pretty good, too.

Serves 4

2 eggs
40g/⅓ cup plain/all purpose flour
100g/2 cups Panko breadcrumbs
20–30 langoustine tails or large prawns, peeled and deveined (defrosted if frozen)
olive oil, for spraying
sea-salt flakes and ground black pepper

PRAWN SKEWERS

Now some might think, 'Feta and prawns? No way!' But this combo has been around for centuries (don't quote me on that as I'm not great at history or geography ... or anything other than cooking really). It's popular in Turkish cooking and elsewhere around the Middle East (again, not great at geography, remember). The feta adds a salty and acidic bite to the sweetness of the prawns. Chef's kiss. It will have your tastebuds tingling.

1 Pat the prawns dry with kitchen paper and season lightly.

2 Warm the olive oil in a saucepan, then add the garlic and fennel seeds. Cook for 30 seconds, until fragrant. Remove from the heat and allow to cool.

3 Heat the air fryer to 200°C/400°F. Toss the prawns in the garlic and fennel and thread them on to the skewers. Place the skewers in the air-fryer basket and cook for 3–4 minutes, until just cooked.

4 Serve the skewers on a platter, season generously with salt and pepper and scatter over the feta, lemon zest and basil. Serve with the lemon wedges on the side.

MY SUGGESTIONS

Of course, you can serve these without the feta, but it's just a really flavourful way of eating these skewers. I would also suggest mopping up any juices with warm, crusty, buttered bread.

Alternatively, scatter the prawns through pasta dishes such as a linguine. Just boil your pasta, then in a deep frying pan on the highest heat, add 400g/2⅔ cups of halved cherry tomatoes, 3 sliced garlic cloves, 1 teaspoon of chilli flakes, 1 tablespoon of olive oil and salt and pepper and cook for around 5–10 minutes, just stirring occasionally to prevent burning. Then, stir through 1 tablespoon of mascarpone or cream cheese. Once the pasta is ready, add the pasta to the sauce with a ladleful of pasta cooking water. Add the air-fryer cooked prawns and serve with a side salad and garlic bread (see page 168). The perfect weekday dinner.

Serves 4

330g/12oz prawns, peeled and deveined (defrosted if frozen)
60ml/¼ cup olive oil
2 garlic cloves, sliced
2 teaspoons fennel seeds
100g/1 cup feta, crumbled
1 lemon, zested and cut into 4 wedges
30g/¼ cup basil, roughly chopped
sea-salt flakes and ground black pepper

You will also need
8–12 wooden skewers, soaked for 1 hour in hot water

GARLIC PRAWNS

Garlic, garlic, garlic. Just like potatoes, garlic is something I couldn't live without. Match that with perfectly succulent prawns and without any hassle you have a flavour-first winning meal.

1   Heat the air fryer to 180°C/350°F.

2   Make a roasted garlic butter. Slice the top off the garlic bulb, keeping the bulb intact, and wrap the bulb in foil. Place the wrapped bulb in the air-fryer basket and cook for about 20 minutes, until soft and smelling sweet.

3   Once the garlic is cooked, squeeze the soft flesh into a small bowl, then add the butter and parsley and season generously.

4   Pat the prawns dry with kitchen paper and season lightly. Thread the prawns on to the skewers and liberally brush on the garlic butter.

5   Place the prawns in the air-fryer basket and cook for 3–4 minutes, until just cooked. Serve piled on top of slices of the toasted ciabatta, with any extra garlic butter for dolloping and dunking.

MY SUGGESTIONS

I think garlic on garlic is the way to go with this dish, so prior to cooking the prawns, make some garlic bread (see page 168) and just keep it to one side while you make your garlic prawns.

Also try making prawn tacos: slap the prawns on some tortillas, slather with guac, pico de gallo (see page 94) and add a dollop of soured cream.

What's great about this prawn recipe (and the others) is that any leftovers are perfect with pasta. Just be sure to fully reheat the prawns before serving.

Serves 4

½ garlic bulb
100g/7 tablespoons
    butter, melted
15g/⅓ cup flat-leaf
    parsley, leaves
    and stems roughly
    chopped
330g/12oz prawns,
    peeled and deveined
    (defrosted if frozen)
1 ciabatta, halved and
    toasted
salt and ground black
    pepper

You will also need
8–12 wooden skewers,
    soaked for 1 hour in
    hot water

PRAWNS PIL PIL

When I say I was the kid at school who went to only Spain on my holidays, I mean I WENT TO ONLY SPAIN and one of my favourite dishes while I was there was prawns pil pil. It's so simple yet so delicious – spicy chilli, savoury, garlic goodness.

1 Heat the air fryer to 130°C/270°F.

2 Get a deep tray or pan that fits in your air fryer. Tip the garlic cloves into it along with the olive oil and chillies. Cover with foil and cook for 10–20 minutes, until the garlic has softened and is just beginning to colour. Remove and allow to cool, then stir through the paprika. Pour out half the confit garlic oil and keep to one side for a rainy day. (It will keep in a sterilised jar in the fridge for up to 6 months.)

3 Heat the air fryer to 200°C/400°F.

4 Pat the prawns dry with kitchen paper and season them lightly. Toss the seasoned prawns in the tray/pan with the garlic oil and leave to marinate for 10 minutes before adding the sherry vinegar.

5 Place the tray/pan back in the air-fryer basket and cook for 5–7 minutes, until just cooked.

6 Taste and adjust the seasoning as necessary, then scatter over the chopped parsley and serve with crusty bread.

Serves 4

8 garlic cloves, peeled
200ml/generous ¾ cup olive oil
4 dried bird's-eye chillies
1 teaspoon smoked paprika
2 teaspoons sherry vinegar
330g/12oz prawns, peeled and deveined (defrosted if frozen)
30g/⅔ cup flat-leaf parsley, leaves and stems roughly chopped
crusty bread, to serve

MY SUGGESTIONS

You could serve these alongside a tapas feast, with red wine chorizo bites, a Spanish omelette, some serrano ham, padrón peppers and a little paella. It will make you feel like you are on holiday again and again.

Bonus meal: you can turn any leftovers into a quick tomato and prawn spaghetti supper. Warm 2 tablespoons of garlic oil in a frying pan. Add 250g/scant 1 cup of chopped tomatoes and cook down. Stir through the leftover prawns and some cooked spaghetti, adding a splash of pasta cooking water to create a sauce. Bingo!

PRAWNS IN FILO

There is something about crispy, crunchy filo pastry that just does things to me. Then, to fill it with delicate prawn ... it's a match made in heaven. Best served piping hot, dipped in sweet chilli sauce on a summer's evening with an array of other picky bits.

1   Heat the air fryer to 180°C/350°F.

2   To prepare the prawns, for each prawn, remove the head and the shell from the body, leaving the tail intact. Use a sharp knife to remove the intestines. Once you have prepared them all, toss them in the soy sauce.

3   Cut a sheet of filo pastry in half lengthways, so that you end up with two long strips. Brush each half with a little sesame oil. Lay a prawn on the short edge of the pastry, so that the tail is sticking out over the top. Fold the pastry over the prawn and roll up into a neat parcel. Brush with sesame oil and place on a lined baking tray. Repeat with the remaining prawns and pastry.

4   Place the prawns in the air-fryer basket and cook for 5-7 minutes, until crisp and golden.

Serves 4 as a snack

*400g/14oz shell-on
   king prawns
2 tablespoons dark
   soy sauce
135g/5oz filo pastry
sesame oil, for brushing*

MY SUGGESTIONS

Ideal for dipping, these are great with some sweet chilli sauce, spicy chilli oil, or even a coriander/cilantro and lemongrass sauce. To make this sauce, simply blend together 1 bulb end of lemongrass, 1 garlic clove, a bunch of coriander/cilantro, 1cm/½-inch piece of fresh ginger (grated), 1 teaspoon of white sugar, 1 tablespoon of rice wine vinegar and 2 teaspoons of water to a paste, then drizzle in a neutral oil until you have a sauce. Season and enjoy.

PRAWN TOAST

A must-have if I'm ever ordering a takeaway, and it turns out they are actually delicious made in the air fryer. This is my fresh version packed with herbs, and one to add to the list for the perfect fakeaway night in!

1 Heat the air fryer to 200°C/400°F.

2 Reserve one third of the coriander leaves and roughly chop the remainder with all the stalks. Set aside.

3 Add the chopped coriander, spring onions, ginger, garlic, prawns, egg white and soy sauce to a food processor. Blitz until evenly combined but not completely smooth.

4 Cut the slices of bread into four triangles, spoon the prawn mixture on top and sprinkle with sesame seeds. (If you're using crumpets, it's easiest to leave them whole and slice them afterwards.)

5 Add the prawn toasts to the air-fryer basket, leaving plenty of space between them, and cook for 4–6 minutes, until crisp and golden. Crumpets will need about 5–7 minutes. Sprinkle with the reserved coriander leaves, and slice the crumpets if that's what you've used.

MY SUGGESTIONS

Serve this on a platter of fakeaway dishes that includes spring rolls (see page 154), prawns in filo (see page 103), lemon chicken (see page 31), crispy shredded beef (see page 71) and plenty of sweet chilli sauce to dip in.

Serves 4

15g/½oz coriander/cilantro
3 spring onions, roughly chopped
2cm/¾-inch piece fresh ginger, peeled and roughly chopped
½ garlic clove, roughly chopped
200g/½lb prawns, peeled and deveined (defrosted if frozen)
1 egg white
1–2 teaspoons dark soy sauce
4 slices of slightly stale white bread, or 4 crumpets
1–2 tablespoons toasted sesame seeds

COCONUT SHRIMP

I first had coconut shrimp when I was lucky enough to go to Barbados, and my goodness did it change my life. Ohhh ... the sweet tones of coconut (a real favourite flavour of mine), golden crispiness and thick juicy prawns. It takes me back to being sat on a beach every time I eat it. And hopefully it will do the same to you. You HAVE to try it with the coriander/cilantro dip, but if like me you love it that much, I'd try all the combinations you can think of.

1   Heat the air fryer to 220°C/425°F (or your air fryer's maximum temperature).

2   Pat the prawns dry with kitchen paper and lightly season.

3   Find three shallow bowls. Add the desiccated coconut, breadcrumbs, smoked paprika, cayenne pepper, lime zest, a pinch of salt and a good grind of black pepper to the first and toss together. Crack the eggs into the second bowl and whisk gently, then add the flour to the third.

4   Using one hand for the wet ingredients (eggs) and the other for the dry ingredients (flour and breadcrumbs), one by one, dip the prawns in the flour, then the egg, then the breadcrumbs, to coat fully, and place them on a lined baking tray.

5   Add the prawns to the air-fryer basket, making sure there is plenty of space between them. Cook for 4–5 minutes, turning halfway through, until crisp and golden. (For extra deliciousness do this in batches, depending on the size of your air fryer.) Squeeze over the lime juice and serve straight away.

Serves 4 as a snack (makes about 30)

330g/12oz ready-to-eat prawns (defrosted if frozen)
50g/scant ¾ cup desiccated coconut
50g/½ cup Panko breadcrumbs
½ teaspoon smoked paprika
½ teaspoon cayenne pepper
1 lime, zested and juiced
2 eggs, lightly beaten
50g/heaping ⅓ cup plain/all purpose flour
salt and ground black pepper

MY SUGGESTIONS

These are perfect on their own with a coconut and coriander/cilantro yogurt dip. In a food processor, blend 20g/¾oz of coriander/cilantro and add coconut yogurt (the dairy alternative, not a flavoured yogurt) a tablespoon at a time. Taste and season with salt and lemon juice to get it to your liking. It's simple but really complements the prawns.

SPUDS
& SIDES

BAKED POTATOES

Winter, spring, summer or autumn, the baked potato will be there. But before I break into song, let it be known how much I appreciate a good jacket potato. It is by far one of the most comforting foods on the planet – and, with the right technique, can be cooked perfectly in the air fryer. This is now my go-to technique for cooking a baked spud, as it reduces the amount of time it takes to get that crispy exterior and fluffy centre. I love mine topped with EVERYTHING, but the beauty is you can go with whatever you fancy – chilli, tuna or even cheesy beans.

1   Using a fork, pierce the potatoes all over and rub with oil and salt. Get onto a microwave-safe plate and microwave at 800W for 10 minutes.

2   Heat the air fryer to 170°C/340°F.

3   Put the potatoes in the air-fryer basket for 25–30 minutes, until tender, delicious, fluffy and ready for the filling of your choice. My favourites are below.

MY SUGGESTIONS

Kumpir: A dish from Turkey, this basically throws as much as possible into your jacket potato, and it is AMAZING. I like to have butter (obvs), feta, pickled red cabbage, tinned sweetcorn, olives, ready-made potato salad (yes spud-on-spud action) and some chopped gherkins. Once this has all been safely stuffed in the potato, slather on mayonnaise and ketchup. Life changing.

Chilli cheesy beans: Simple as this – fry half a sliced onion in a frying in a pan with some oil, until softened, then add half a finely grated garlic clove. Add your favourite baked beans, a pinch of chilli flakes, a dash of hot sauce and a little grated cheese. Then butter up your potato and pour on your pimped beans. Sprinkle with another helping of cheese. A feast for kings, that.

The classic: Get some bacon crisping up in a pan (or the air fryer; see page 46). While that's on, open your jacket and mix the inner potato with butter and soured cream. Chop a spring onion and mix that in there as well, saving a little to sprinkle on top. Once the bacon is cooked and crispy, chop it up into little pieces and add it to the potato. Then, get grated cheddar and/or Red Leicester all over that bad boy. Add the remaining spring onion and a dollop of soured cream and you're away.

Serves as many as you need

1 baking potato, or large Maris Piper or Russet potato, per person
vegetable oil, for rubbing
salt

CHIPS

It wouldn't be a Poppy Cooks book without a chip masterclass. I turn to my air fryer friend when I need quick, easy, no-mess chips, and they never let me down.

1   Peel and cut your potatoes into thick chip shapes, about the size of your index finger.

2   Heat the air fryer to 180°C/350°F.

3   In a bowl, toss the chips, oil and salt and mix well, then get them into the air-fryer basket.

4   Cook for 15 minutes, give them a mix and then return to the air fryer and cook for a further 15 minutes, until golden.

Serves 4

6–8 large/long red skin, Maris Piper or Russet potatoes
2 tablespoons vegetable oil
1 teaspoon fine salt

MY SUGGESTIONS

To make fries rather than fat chips, just cut the potatoes into thin French fries. Follow the steps in the same way, except cook for only 10 minutes, then mix, then cook again for another 15 minutes.

Loaded chips or fries are The One, so try these with a classic chilli con carne, smoked cheddar and soured cream combo. For the chilli, fry 250g/9oz of minced beef in a super-hot pan, until browned. Remove the meat from the pan and set aside. Add a chopped onion and brown off, then add in 2 chopped garlic cloves, 1 tablespoon of tomato purée/paste, 2 teaspoons of ground cumin, 2 teaspoons of ground coriander, 2 teaspoons of smoked paprika, 1 teaspoon of cayenne pepper and 1 teaspoon of chilli flakes, and mix well. Add the mince back to the pan, just cover with beef stock and leave to cook on a medium heat until the liquid has almost all been absorbed. Add in a drained tin of red kidney beans, season and serve on top of your chips. Grate over cheese and dollop on soured cream.

Poutine (fries, cheese curd, gravy) is amazing but in the UK we do it better – and it's called 'cheesy chips and gravy'! Just grate some of you favourite cheddar on top of your hot, cooked chips, then pour over a beef gravy (just the one you mix with boiling water will do). It really is that easy to have one of the best meals in all the land.

HASSELBACKS

An underrated potato that I'm desperate to bring back into fashion because they are just SO GOOD! Once you've got the cutting technique down (you'll need two wooden spoons), this potato is crispy and crunchy while still being pillowy and fluffy in the middle. A winning potato.

1   Heat the air fryer to 200°C/400°F.

2   Place a wooden spoon either side of the first potato (along each long side). Now slice across the potato along its length at 2–3mm/¹⁄₁₆-inch intervals, using the spoon handles to stop you cutting all the way through. Repeat with the remaining potatoes.

3   Get the spuds into the air-fryer basket and drizzle the oil all over, then heavily season them with salt.

4   Cook for 20–25 minutes, then add a knob of butter to each potato and return to the fryer for a further 15–20 minutes, until the potatoes are cooked all the way through. (Use a sharp knife to test for doneness – if there is still resistance, keep cooking in 5-minute intervals until they're done.)

MY SUGGESTIONS

Hasselbacks are perfect with most meat and fish dishes and a really fun way to have an apparently plain potato. But, of course, the hasselback can take centre stage, too. Try using differently flavoured butters to enhance the experience. Or glazing them in honey and garlic, sticky soy sauce, or even buffalo sauce for an extra kick.

Serves 6

6 medium-large Maris Piper, Russet or red skin potatoes
1 tablespoon vegetable oil
6 small knobs of butter
sea-salt flakes

ROAST POTATOES

Now we're talking, the reason you're all here, the star of the show, the beautiful roast potato. Believe it or not, I'm no stranger to a roast potato or two (or seven), and I've made it my life's work to ensure you have the best potatoes on your plate every time. With an air fryer, the process is much quicker, which means potato gets to your mouth in half the time – always a good thing. I turn to my air fryer for roast potatoes when it's a quick dinner kinda day. For me, the perfect roast potato has a crispy exterior while still maintaining a beautifully fluffy interior, and this recipe does exactly that.

1   Heat the air fryer to 160°C/325°F.

2   In a mixing bowl, toss the potatoes in the oil and salt, and tip them into the air-fryer basket.

3   Cook for 30 minutes, giving them a proper aggressive toss every 10 minutes, and even poke them with a fork if you want to fluff up the insides further.

4   Increase the heat to 200°C/400°F and cook for a further 6 minutes, until golden and crispy.

MY SUGGESTIONS

Why mess with the best? But, if you have to, try melting 2 tablespoons of either duck fat, goose fat or beef dripping and coating the potatoes in it before you cook them.

Also, once the roasties are cooked, you can add finely grated Parmesan, chopped rosemary, and a sprinkle of olive oil, sea-salt flakes and black pepper.

Serves 2–4, depending on greed

4 Maris Piper, Russet or red skin potatoes, peeled and cut into quarters
2 tablespoons vegetable oil
1 teaspoon fine salt

CRISPY POTATO CUBES

A crispy cube potato is like a roast potato's little sibling. And you get the ultimate crunch because these are so small and delicious. I've suggested a few combos to make these next level but they're great as they are, too.

1   Get your potatoes in a mixing bowl, and mix with the oil and salt.

2   Heat the air fryer to 180°C/350°F.

3   Get your potatoes into the air-fryer basket and cook for 20 minutes. Give them a good shake.

4   Turn the air fryer up to 190°C/375°F and cook for a further 10 minutes, then they are ready to serve.

Serves 4

4–6 red skin, Maris Piper or Russet potatoes, scrubbed and cut into 2cm/¾-inch cubes
2 tablespoons vegetable oil
1 teaspoon fine salt

MY SUGGESTIONS

To make garlic, honey and mustard crispy cubes, simply get a garlic bulb and cut just the top off it. Place the bulb in foil and drizzle with oil and salt. Fold up the foil and scrunch it around the bulb. Add this to the air fryer for the first 20 minutes of cooking the potatoes. Once ready, remove from the foil and carefully squeeze the soft cloves into a mixing bowl with 1–2 tablespoons of runny honey and 1–2 teaspoons of wholegrain mustard. Mix well and when the spuds are done, toss them in the garlic-honey-mustard paste and dig in.

Or try tossing the crispy cubes in a handful of chopped parsley, a sprig of rosemary leaves, finely chopped, a handful of finely grated Parmesan and a finely grated garlic clove.

Or go very bistro and drizzle the cooked potato cubes in some truffle oil and finely grated Parmesan.

WEDGES

For years I thought everyone called potato wedges 'potato wedgies'. These are like a chunkier relative of the chip and make for a lovely side dish to any meal.

1   Clean and chop your potatoes into wedges. To do this, I cut them in half lengthways and then in half lengthways again. Then, with the insides of the potatoes looking up, cut the super-thin edge and repeat. You should get between 8 and 12 wedges out of 1 potato.

2   Heat the air fryer to 180°C/350°F.

3   Add the wedges to a large mixing bowl along with the oil and salt, toss well to coat then get these into the air-fryer basket and cook for 15 minutes.

4   Turn the wedges over and turn up the air fryer up to 200°C/400°F. Cook for a final 10 minutes, until golden and crispy, and serve.

MY SUGGESTIONS

For an extra flavour hit, try adding a spice mix of 2 teaspoons of smoked paprika, and 1 teaspoon each of garlic powder, dried oregano, onion powder, ground coriander, ground cumin and chilli flakes to the wedges in the air-fryer basket around 5 minutes before they are cooked. This will add another layer of flavour. Or, try your own version of a spice mix – let your imagination run wild.

Serves 4

4 large Maris Piper, Russet or red skin potatoes
2 tablespoons vegetable oil
1–2 teaspoons fine salt
ground black pepper

POTATO SKINS

Order me these in any restaurant and I'll be your best friend. The best thing about potato skins is the ability to customise with toppings and get a different mouthful with every skin. Air fryers make them extra crunchy too.

1 Heat the air fryer to 170°C/340°F. Rub oil all over the spuds and then sprinkle them with salt.

2 Pop the potatoes into the air-fryer basket and cook for 20 minutes, then up the temperature to 200°C/400°F for a further 15 minutes, until the flesh is tender.

3 Remove the potatoes from the basket and cut each one in half. Scoop out the flesh into a bowl, reserving the skins, and set aside.

4 Separate out one quarter of the flesh into a different bowl (see notes for what to do with the remainder – waste no potato!) and mix it with the butter and almost all of the cheese (leave enough for sprinkling just before cooking). Season with salt and pepper. Then spoon equal amounts of the cheesy potato back into the skins.

5 Sprinkle the potato skins with pancetta and the remaining cheese and return them to the air fryer.

6 Cook for 10 minutes, until the pancetta is cooked and the skins are crispy. Remove and garnish with the spring onion.

MY SUGGESTIONS

For a veggie option, replace the bacon with slices of cooked chestnut mushrooms. Or try vegetarian smoked cheese, with red peppers and caramelised onions. If you're vegan, try vegan almond cream cheese with sun-dried tomatoes.

Otherwise, try shredded chicken in buffalo hot sauce and blue cheese.

You will have some leftover cooked potato and you can do plenty with this. Try using it to make gnocchi (mix with flour, egg and Parmesan, or if you want a full recipe, check out my first book *wink wink*), to top a pie, to make the fish cakes from page 90; or just serve as a side as mashed potato.

Serves 4

4 Maris Piper, Russet, red skin or baking potatoes, pierced all over with a fork
vegetable oil, for rubbing
2 tablespoons butter
100g/1 cup mixed grated cheddar and mozzarella
100g/1 cup diced smoked pancetta
salt and ground black pepper
4 spring onions, thinly sliced, to garnish

HASH BROWNS

A hash brown is the morning glory of the potato world. Serve these up with the air fryer sausage patties (see page 48) and recreate an infamous Big Gold Shiny M fast-food breakfast that'll go down a treat.

1   Soak the grated potato in cold water for 10 minutes.

2   A handful of potato at a time, dry the grated potato in a clean tea towel, squeezing to get out the excess moisture. Tip the dry potato into a large mixing bowl.

3   Add the egg and cornflour to the bowl and season heavily with salt and pepper. Mix well until everything is combined.

4   Heat the air fryer to 200°C/400°F and spray the air-fryer basket with oil.

5   Divide the mixture into four equal portions and, using your hands, use each portion to make a patty, like the classic hash-brown shape.

6   Add the patties to the air-fryer basket, spacing them apart, and spray again with oil. Cook for 15 minutes until golden and crispy.

MY SUGGESTIONS

These have to be served on a full breakfast – we are talking sausages, bacon, tomato, mushrooms, baked beans, black pudding, fried bread and some fried eggs. It's perfect!

Or, you could try serving with poached eggs, sautéed spinach and hollandaise sauce (the recipe is in my first book).

Serves 4

3 Maris Piper, Russet or red skin potatoes, peeled and coarsely grated
1 egg, lightly whisked
1 tablespoon cornflour/ cornstarch
vegetable oil, for spraying
salt and ground black pepper

SWEET POTATO CUBES

These cubes are a time-saver and are a nice twist to your average sweet potato. They literally go with anything, including any of the meat or fish dishes in this book. Try them all and let me know which was best!

1 Heat the air fryer to 200°C/400°F.

2 Warm a small frying pan over a medium heat, add the cumin seeds and cook for 30 seconds, until fragrant. Tip the toasted seeds into a mortar and crush them with the pestle. Set aside.

3 Toss the potato pieces in the olive oil and the toasted, crushed cumin and season generously.

4 Place the sweet potato cubes in the air-fryer basket, making sure that there's plenty of space between each (you might have to do this in batches, depending on the size of your air fryer). Cook for 25–30 minutes, shaking a couple of times during cooking, until crisp and golden.

Serves 4

1 teaspoon cumin seeds
2 large sweet potatoes, peeled and cut into 2cm/¾-inch pieces
1 tablespoon olive oil
sea-salt flakes and ground black pepper

MY SUGGESTIONS

Have this as a snack with dips – roasted garlic aïoli, coriander/cilantro chutney, habanero salsa and spicy tomato salsa are top choices.

Level up with pink pickled onions (see page 64), coriander/cilantro, feta, toasted chickpeas, or anything else you fancy.

Use these as an alternative for any meal when you'd usually have a potato side (although, an alternative to regular potatoes – how dare you?!).

CRISPY KALE

People have been hating on kale ever since it's been caught up in fad diets, green smoothies and January detoxes. It's time we stop underestimating the deliciousness of the humble kale. I'm here to reclaim kale as a tasty, flavoursome side that will have you rethinking those times you've ever bad-mouthed it. The key to delicious kale? Crisping it up in the air fryer. Crispy kale is delicious on any meal, but I personally love it atop a Sunday roast, seasoned to perfection and giving added texture to your plate. Try this recipe at least once, and thank me later. #JusticeForKale

1   Heat the air fryer to 150°C/300°F.

2   In a large mixing bowl, toss the torn leaves with the olive oil and a sprinkling of sea-salt flakes.

3   Add the kale to the air-fryer basket in a single layer that isn't overcrowded (for optimum deliciousness do this in batches, depending on the size of your air fryer). Cook for 7–8 minutes, stirring halfway through, until crisp. The kale will crisp up as it cools, so don't worry if it's not completely crispy when you take it out of the air fryer.

MY SUGGESTIONS

You can adapt this recipe by swapping the kale for cavolo nero and adding toasted nuts to the crispy greens once cooked. It's a really great snack for the health conscious, or as a side to a meal.

Serves 4

250g/9oz kale, leaves and stalks separated, leaves torn into bite-sized pieces
2 tablespoons olive oil
sea-salt flakes

CHILLI HONEY ROASTED PARSNIPS

The little kick you get from the chilli, balanced against the sweet honey, makes for a delicious twist on your everyday parsnips. They're always pushed aside for a carrot or broccoli, but it's time to amp up your parsnip game to let them shine on your plate.

1   Get the honey and chilli flakes in a small saucepan and warm them up together until the honey has turned a slight red. Add the garlic and set aside.

2   Heat the air fryer to 180°C/350°F.

3   Put the parsnips in a bowl and drizzle over the melted butter and the chilli honey. Toss them together so the parsnips are fully coated (don't get rid of any honey left in the bowl as we will use it to glaze later).

4   Get the parsnips into the air-fryer basket and cook for 8 minutes, then give them a toss and glaze with any of the chilli honey that was remaining in the bowl.

5   Return the parsnips to the air fryer for another 8 minutes, until they are well glazed and golden. If you think at this point they aren't tender and cooked through, keep cooking, checking on them in 4-minute intervals. Sprinkle with chilli flakes to serve.

MY SUGGESTIONS

You can make a larger batch of the chilli honey if, like me, you LOVE it. It will keep in a sterilised, airtight jar for 3 months and is delicious drizzled over pizzas, pasta or chicken, or served with cheese boards, or anything really.

To make this dish vegan, replace the honey with maple syrup and use a dairy-free vegan alternative butter.

Serves 4

2 tablespoons runny honey
1 tablespoon chilli flakes, plus extra to sprinkle
1 garlic clove, crushed
4 fattish parsnips, trimmed, peeled and quartered
1 teaspoon melted butter
salt and ground black pepper

ASPARAGUS

There's something about asparagus that just makes you feel dead posh. You don't have to tell your dinner-party guests that it only took a few minutes in the air fryer.

1   Heat the air fryer to 200°C/400°F.

2   Toss the asparagus with the olive oil.

3   Place the oiled asparagus in the air-fryer basket for 6–8 minutes, turning halfway through, until just tender. Season generously with sea salt and ground black pepper.

MY SUGGESTIONS

Serve with butter, hollandaise or roasted garlic aïoli for dipping. Or serve alongside any of the main dishes in this book as an easy side dish that leaves you feeling quite fancy!

Serves 4

500g/about 1lb asparagus, woody ends snapped off
1 tablespoon olive oil
sea-salt flakes and ground black pepper

SPRING ONIONS

Now, I am a fan of a cooked spring onion. We used to serve them in some of the restaurants I worked in. They are so tasty and add an easy element of onion and finesse to any dish.

1   Heat the air fryer to 180°C/350°F.

2   Toss the onions in a bowl with the oil and season with salt and pepper.

3   Get them into the air-fryer basket for 5 minutes, give them a toss and then cook for a further 5 minutes, until cooked through and slightly crisp on the outside.

MY SUGGESTIONS

These are delicious served with fish dishes, with a white wine sauce, or with rich meat dishes, as they cut through the depth of a dish.

Serves 4

8 spring onions, trimmed, washed and tidied
1 tablespoon vegetable oil
salt and ground black pepper

CORN-ON-THE-COB

Smother this in butter and the rest is history. No more explanation needed.

1 Heat the air fryer to 200°C/400°F.

2 Toss the corns in a bowl with the olive oil, then place them in the air-fryer basket, making sure there is plenty of space between each.

3 Cook for 20–25 minutes, turning them a couple of times, until they are tender and crisp at the edges.

4 Season generously with salt and pepper, and a knob of butter if you like.

MY SUGGESTIONS

Try these cobs with differently flavoured butters: herb butter, chilli butter, lemon butter or honey butter all work. Just get some softened butter (around 100g/7 tablespoons) and mix in as much or as little of the flavour you want. Roll the flavoured butter into a sausage shape in cling film or set it in a container and leave it in the fridge until it's hardened up again. The longer you leave it, the more flavour it takes on.

Serves 4

4 corn-on-the-cobs, patted dry with kitchen paper
1–2 tablespoons olive oil
25g/2 tablespoons butter (optional)
sea-salt flakes and ground black pepper

CORN RIBS

Corn ribs were a trend on TikTok – but, unlike many other TikTok fads, this one had legs ... or ribs ... they are actually delicious. It's a beautiful veggie side, starter or even main, and enters the land of food I love – fun to pick up and eat as much as is tasty.

1 Warm a small frying pan over a medium heat, add the cumin and coriander seeds and toast for 30 seconds, until fragrant. Tip out the toasted seeds into a mortar and crush them with a pestle. Add the paprika, oregano, sugar and cinnamon and season generously with salt and pepper.

2 Using a very sharp, heavy knife, trim the ends of the cobs to make them flat. Stand each cob on a flat end and cut it in half lengthways. Warning – this is quite difficult!

3 Then, cut the halves lengthways into wedges, each about 4 kernels of corn wide. Drizzle the 'ribs' with olive oil and toss them with the spice mixture.

4 Heat the air fryer to 200°C/400°F. Get the ribs into the air-fryer basket and cook for 20–25 minutes, until charred at the edges.

5 While the corn is cooking, mix the butter with the lime zest and some of the juice, to taste. Season generously.

6 Once the ribs are cooked, dot them with the zesty butter and serve them with the lime wedges for squeezing over.

Serves 4

1 teaspoon cumin seeds
1 teaspoon coriander seeds
½ teaspoon smoked paprika
1 teaspoon dried oregano
1 teaspoon dark brown soft sugar
pinch of ground cinnamon
4 corn-on-the-cobs
olive oil
60g/4 tablespoons butter, melted
2 limes, 1 zested and juiced and 1 cut into wedges
sea-salt flakes and ground black pepper

MY SUGGESTIONS

For the ultimate buffet, serve these up with your dip and you're good to go alongside your choice of air-fryer sides.

Add a pinch of chipotle chilli flakes to the spice mixture, if you like.

CHESTNUT AND BACON SPROUTS

Sprouts are underrated and can be such a delicious vegetable side. When they are cooked right, and not pure mush, they add texture, flavour and colour to any dish.

1 Heat the air fryer to 180°C/350°F.

2 In a large bowl, mix the butter with the sprouts, season with salt and pepper and place in the air-fryer basket. Just chuck over the bacon lardons.

3 Cook for 5 minutes then add in the chestnuts. Cook for another 5–10 minutes, checking at 5-minute intervals until cooked to your liking.

MY SUGGESTIONS

You can, of course, make these vegetarian by removing the bacon and make them vegan by doing the same and using a dairy-free vegan alternative butter.

Sprouts are so high in nutrients and folic acid that they are really good for you, so don't be shy. Try having them with stuffed chicken breasts (see page 34) or a steak. I mean, obviously, these are also perfect served on a Sunday roast or in the festive season for Thanksgiving and Christmas.

Serves 4

50g/3 tablespoons butter, melted
500g/about 1lb fresh or frozen Brussels sprouts (if fresh, cut in half)
100g/scant 1 cup bacon lardons
50g/⅓ cup pre-cooked chestnuts, chopped
sea-salt flakes and ground black pepper

HONEY ROAST CARROTS

This one goes out to all the lost carrots over the years that have been just cut into rounds and boiled. I'm sorry you went out like that. We will do better. Here's to more carrots being roasted in honey and going out in style. They deserve it.

1   Heat the air fryer to 180°C/350°F.

2   Get the carrots in the air-fryer basket and spray them with the vegetable oil. Then cook them for 10 minutes.

3   Meanwhile, in a microwaveable bowl, melt the honey and butter together for about 30 seconds, until liquidy, then season well.

4   When the carrots have been in the air fryer for 10 minutes, tip them into the honey and butter mixture and mix well so that they are all coated, then pop them back into the air fryer for a further 10 minutes, until sticky, glazed and tender. Depending on the size of your carrots, you may need to cook them for a little longer, so cook in 5-minute intervals until tender.

MY SUGGESTIONS

To make this dish vegan, replace the honey with maple syrup and use a dairy-free vegan alternative butter.

You could add 1 crushed garlic clove to the honey and butter mix for an extra flavour hit.

Serves 4

*4 carrots, peeled
    and sliced in half
    lengthways
vegetable oil, for
    spraying
2 tablespoons runny
    honey
1 teaspoon butter
salt and ground black
    pepper*

LONGSTEM BROCCOLI

This broccoli dish is the perfect accompaniment to fish, roast dinners or pies. It's so versatile and the air fryer will get it on your plate quickly and ready to go.

1   Heat the air fryer to 180°C/350°F.

2   Toss the broccoli in a bowl with the olive oil. Place the coated broccoli in the air-fryer basket and cook for 7–9 minutes, until tender and charred at the edges. Season generously.

MY SUGGESTIONS

Elevate the humble broccoli by adding a soy glaze and crushed, toasted peanuts; or a tahini dressing, pomegranate seeds and toasted almond flakes.

Serves 4

400g/about 1lb longstem broccoli/ broccolini, woody ends trimmed
1 tablespoon olive oil
salt

CAULIFLOWER WINGS

Don't sleep on cauliflower. These buffalo wings are delicious and come out perfectly in the air fryer. Use this dish to get some veg in your otherwise meat-filled BBQ, or to convert cauli-hating kids. Either way, always a treat.

1   First, make the Korean BBQ sauce by getting the onion into a medium saucepan with a splash of oil and cooking over a medium heat for about 10 minutes, until translucent.

2   Add the red chilli, garlic and ginger and cook for 2–3 minutes, until fragrant, then add the remaining sauce ingredients and 200ml/ generous ¾ cup of water. Bring to the boil, then simmer until reduced by half. Remove from the heat and use a stick blender to blitz until smooth. Taste to check the flavours and adjust as necessary. It should be a balance of sweet, salty, spicy and sour. Set aside for later.

3   Tip the sesame seeds into a dry frying pan over a medium heat. Toast for 30 seconds then immediately tip them on to a plate to cool.

4   Bring a large saucepan of salted water to the boil. Add the cauliflower and cook for 4 minutes, until just tender. Drain and refresh in cold water.

5   Heat the air fryer to 180°C/350°F. Find three shallow bowls. Tip the eggs into one bowl, the flour into the second bowl and the breadcrumbs into the third. Lightly season the breadcrumbs.

6   Using one hand for the wet ingredients (eggs) and the other for the dry ingredients (flour and breadcrumbs), toss a few pieces of cauliflower in the flour, then the egg, then the breadcrumbs, and place on a lined baking tray. Repeat with the remaining cauliflower.

7   Lightly drizzle or spray the cauliflower wings with sesame oil and place in the air-fryer basket, leaving plenty of space between them. Cook for 10–15 minutes, turning once, until crisp and golden.

8   Warm the sauce and toss through the cooked cauliflower. Tip the coated cauliflower into a big serving dish and scatter over the spring onion and toasted sesame seeds.

MY SUGGESTIONS

You could finish the wings with some sliced red chilli or finely chopped chives, too.

Serves 4

2 tablespoons sesame seeds
1 cauliflower, broken into bite-sized pieces
2–3 eggs, lightly whisked (how much egg you need will depend on the size of your cauliflower)
50g/heaping ⅓ cup plain/ all purpose flour
100g/2 cups Panko breadcrumbs
sesame oil, for drizzling or spraying
3 spring onions, finely sliced
salt

For the Korean BBQ sauce
1 onion, finely chopped
splash of olive oil
1 red chilli, deseeded and finely chopped
3 garlic cloves, finely chopped
50g/3½-inch piece fresh ginger, peeled and finely chopped
2 tablespoons runny honey or agave syrup
3 tablespoons dark soy sauce
2 tablespoons gochujang
2 tablespoons rice wine vinegar
splash of vegan fish sauce

DIPPY EGGS AND SOLDIERS

Wait ... a dippy egg? In the air fryer? You heard right! Prepare to have your mind blown in all the right ways when you cook this for yourself and enjoy a delicious bit of dipping. Go tell your friends to throw their eggs in the air fryer next time, too.

1   Heat your air fryer to 130°C/270°F.

2   Get your eggs into the air-fryer basket and cook them for 10 minutes for jammy-yolked eggs, 15 minutes for hard 'boiled' eggs and 20 minutes for extremely hard 'boiled' eggs.

3   Use straight away for dippy eggs or plunge straight into iced water if you want to peel them and use them as hard-boiled eggs.

4   Serve with toasted buttered soldiers from the crusty bread.

Serves as many as you need

as many medium eggs as you want per person
a few slices of crusty, toasted bread per person
butter, for spreading

MY SUGGESTIONS

If you're not eating them just as they are, use these eggs to top salads for extra heartiness. If you like, you can soy-stain them for a ramen or rice bowl by cooling them in iced water, peeling them and then leaving them in a container of seasoned (ginger, garlic, chilli, spring onion and rice wine) soy sauce overnight. This adds so much flavour and an amazing dark colouration all the way around the outside of the egg.

Or, try making devilled eggs – cook the eggs for 15 minutes, cool them in an ice bath, then peel them and cut them in half. Scoop out the yolks, and mix with mayo, a few dashes of tabasco and some chopped spring onion and then spoon the mixture back into the hollows in the egg whites. It's so old school it's actually cool.

GARLIC MUSHROOMS

Garlic and mushroom really is a match made in heaven. I'd even be tempted to make these up as a snack, just in a bowl, nibbling on them one by one. Or you can serve these up with some air-fryer bacon, sausage and egg for the ultimate air-fryer brekkie.

1   Heat the air fryer to 180°C/350°F.

2   Beat the garlic and salt into the butter, and season with black pepper.

3   Turn your mushrooms upside down, then dot the undersides of the caps with the garlic butter and sprinkle over the thyme leaves.

4   Get the mushrooms into the air-fryer basket and cook for 8–10 minutes, until tender. Sit on top of a piece of toast, if you like, and season generously.

MY SUGGESTIONS

You need these mushrooms alongside a good ol' chunk of steak, or just as part of a cooked breakfast (with the hash browns on page 125, too).

Spice up your butter by adding chilli flakes, or use confit garlic if you have some leftover from the recipe on page 100.

Swap out the thyme for chopped flat-leaf parsley, sage or oregano.

Serves 4 as a snack or part of bigger breakfast

1 garlic clove, crushed
½ teaspoon sea-salt flakes, plus extra to season
50g/3 tablespoons butter, softened
1 portobello mushroom per person
4 thyme sprigs, leaves picked
4 slices of toast (optional)
ground black pepper

STUFFED PEPPERS

A beautiful main dish when you're fancying a meat-free day, doing Veganuary (use vegan butter) or if you have a veggie friend coming round for dinner. Tasty with a bit of spice and you don't miss any meat!

1   Warm 2 tablespoons of the olive oil and the knob of butter in a medium saucepan. Add the cumin seeds and cook for 30 seconds, until fragrant. Add the onion and cook on a medium–low heat for about 10 minutes, until translucent and lightly golden.

2   While the onion is cooking, tip the rice into a saucepan of salted water, bring to the boil and cook for 4 minutes, then drain and refresh in cold water.

3   Once the onions are cooked, remove the pan from the heat. Add the par-boiled rice, along with the allspice, Aleppo pepper, chopped tomato or tomato purée and half the parsley, and season generously.

4   Heat the air fryer to 180°C/350°F.

5   Make a slit down the length of a pepper, starting at the top and stopping about 2cm/¾ inch from the bottom, so that you have a pouch. Carefully remove the seeds and pith and rub with a little of the remaining olive oil. Fill the pocket with one quarter of the rice mixture and gently push the edges together. Repeat with the remaining peppers and rice mixture.

6   Get the peppers into the air-fryer basket, making sure there is space between each, and cook for 20–30 minutes, until beginning to char.

7   Sprinkle the peppers with the toasted walnuts, the remaining parsley and a big sprinkling of Aleppo pepper. Serve individually or on a big serving platter.

MY SUGGESTIONS

This is my muhammara-inspired stuffed pepper. You could add crumbled feta, labneh or garlic and lemon yogurt dressing (just add 1 crushed garlic clove and lemon juice to yogurt to taste) to the stuffing, if you wanted.

You could use other soft herbs – coriander/cilantro, chervil, chives and dill would all work well.

Serves 4

3 tablespoons olive oil
knob of butter
1 teaspoon cumin seeds
1 onion, finely chopped
200g/1 cup basmati rice, rinsed until the water runs clear
½–1 teaspoon ground allspice, to taste
1–2 teaspoons Aleppo pepper, to taste, plus extra to sprinkle
2 tomatoes, deseeded and finely chopped or 1 tablespoon tomato purée/paste
30g/⅔ cup flat-leaf parsley, leaves and stems roughly chopped
4 romano peppers (if you can't find romano peppers, use regular red peppers instead)
40g/⅓ cup walnuts, toasted and roughly chopped
sea-salt flakes and ground black pepper

ONION BHAJIS

For me, an onion bhaji is all about that mouthwatering crispiness, and the air fryer achieves that perfectly. Lashings of mango chutney and I'm a very happy girl.

1   In a bowl, mix together the onion, garlic, ginger, melted vegan spread, chilli flakes, turmeric, curry powder, both flours, and the chopped coriander and a pinch of salt. Add just enough water, a sprinkle at a time, until it binds together in a thick mass.

2   Heat the air fryer to 200°C/400°F.

3   Divide your bhaji mixture into 8 equal portions and form each into a roundish, domed disc or slightly flattened ball.

4   Place 4 of the bhajis in the air-fryer basket, spacing them well apart, and spray them generously with oil. Cook for 7 minutes, then turn the bhajis over and give them another good spray. Cook for a further 5 minutes, or until they are golden and crispy on the outside but soft in the middle. Repeat with the remaining bhajis.

MY SUGGESTIONS

A plate of these and with a side of yogurt and mango chutney for dipping makes for a delicious starter for any dinner party, birthday dinner or even just a Thursday night tea.

Serves 4

1 red onion, sliced
2 garlic cloves, chopped
1 teaspoon peeled and chopped fresh ginger
1 tablespoon melted vegan spread
1 teaspoon chilli flakes
1 teaspoon ground turmeric
1 teaspoon mild curry powder
1 tablespoon plain/all purpose flour (use rice flour if you're gluten-free)
3 tablespoons gram/chickpea flour
20g/heaping ⅓ cup coriander/cilantro, leaves and stems chopped
vegetable oil, for spraying
salt

VEGAN FRITTERS

I try to have a meat-free day each week and these fritters are the perfect lunch. A bit of sauce on the side and you're on to a winner. These little fried veggie patties are a great way to use up everything in the fridge as well, so give them a go next time you need to get rid of some veg!

1 Mix together all the ingredients (except the veg oil) in a bowl until well combined. Adjust the liquidity or dryness of the fritters by adding a drop more milk or a touch more flour at a time until you have wet, dough-like consistency.

2 Spray the base of the air fryer basket with oil and heat it to 180°C/350°F.

3 Divide the batter equally into 8 or so flat fritters. Pop 4 fritters into the basket, leaving space between each (do this in smaller batches, depending on the size of your air fryer).

4 Cook for 5 minutes then spray with oil again and turn over the fritters. Cook for a further 10 minutes, until golden and crisp. Repeat with the remaining fritters.

MY SUGGESTIONS

Plate these up with a crispy side salad and some ranch dressing. They make such a fun lunch and you can get the whole family involved in the prep.

You can use any veg you have, or anything in season, but a good starting point is 1 thinly sliced spring onion, 1 grated courgette, 1 grated carrot, and 1 small tin of sweetcorn, drained. Grate, drain or chop other veg to a small, manageable size.

Serves 4

about 500g/5 cups mixed, grated vegetables (see notes for inspo)
20g/1 tablespoon vegan spread
50ml/3 tablespoons oat or almond milk, plus extra if needed
100g/heaping ¾ cup gram/chickpea flour, plus extra if needed
2 garlic cloves, chopped
1 teaspoon finely grated fresh ginger (no need to peel)
20g/heaping ⅓ cup chopped herbs, such as flat-leaf parsley
vegetable oil, for spraying
salt and ground black pepper

ROAST MED VEG

Roasted Mediterranean vegetables are that go-to side when you want to save time but still want something that feels healthy and fresh. The best thing about making them in an air fryer is that you can throw it all in and it turns out absolutely delicious.

1   Heat the air fryer to 200°C/400°F.

2   Toss the aubergine with 1 tablespoon of the olive oil and a little salt. Pop into the air-fryer basket and cook for 20 minutes, until tender.

3   Meanwhile, get the onion wedges, oregano, thyme, tomatoes and broccoli into a large bowl and sprinkle with another tablespoon of the olive oil. Season with salt and pepper and toss to combine.

4   To make a dressing, whisk together the 3 remaining tablespoons of olive oil, along with the lemon juice, garlic and chilli flakes (if using), and season.

5   After the aubergine has had its 20 minutes, push it to one side in the basket and tip in the vegetables. Cook for a further 5–7 minutes, until the veg are just tender.

6   Allow to cool slightly, then transfer to a dish and drizzle over the dressing, crumble over the feta, and add the basil leaves and lemon zest.

MY SUGGESTIONS

Swap around the vegetables, depending on what you have to hand or what's in season.

For extra deliciousness, marinate the feta in olive oil, toasted fennel seeds, ground pepper and rosemary before crumbling it over.

Med veg are great with an array of meats – particularly chicken thighs (see page 24). Or – plot twist – this combo is great with a Sunday roast, such as roast lamb (see page 63). (Don't knock it till you've tried it.)

Serves 4

2 aubergines/eggplants, cut into 2–3cm/1-inch pieces
5 tablespoons olive oil
1 red onion, cut into 1cm/½-inch wedges, keeping the root intact
2 oregano sprigs, leaves picked
2 thyme sprigs, leaves picked
250g/1⅔ cups cherry tomatoes
250g/9oz longstem broccoli/broccolini
1 lemon, zested and juiced
¼ garlic clove, crushed
½ teaspoon chilli flakes (optional)
100g/1 cup feta, crumbled
25g/1 cup basil, leaves picked
sea-salt flakes and ground black pepper

VEGGIE SPRING ROLLS

A spring roll makes sense in the air fryer because you'll achieve that perfect crisp that is so satisfying. Try shredding any veg you have in the fridge to mix it up, or even add a bit of shredded chicken or beef, if you fancy.

1   Soak the vermicelli noodles in warm water until softened, then drain and add to a large mixing bowl. Add the carrots, spring onions, garlic, ginger, mint, bean sprouts, soy sauce and sesame oil to the bowl and toss everything together.

2   To assemble the spring rolls, mix a little flour and water together to make a smooth paste. Lay one spring roll wrapper out on a clean surface and cover the rest with a damp tea towel. Add about 1 tablespoonful of mixture to the centre of the wrapper, just below the middle. Fold the bottom edge over the filling, then fold the sides over the top, so you have a rough rectangle forming a sort of envelope. Roll up the wrapper tightly into a neat sausage shape around the filling and seal the edge with a little flour-water paste. Brush with oil and place on a lined baking tray, then repeat with the remaining mixture and wrappers.

3   Heat the air fryer to 200°C/400°F.

4   Place about 4 spring rolls in the air-fryer basket, making sure there is plenty of space between them, and cook for 15–17 minutes, until crisp and golden. Repeat with the remaining spring rolls and serve hot.

MY SUGGESTIONS

Perfect for a snack, in a picnic or for a full-on buffet. Serve with a side of sweet chilli sauce for dipping.

Makes 10

100g/4oz vermicelli rice noodles
200g/2 cups carrots, julienned or grated
3 spring onions, julienned
¼ garlic clove, finely chopped
3cm/1¼-inch piece fresh ginger, peeled, julienned or finely sliced
15g/heaping ¼ cup mint, leaves picked and torn
150g/2 cups bean sprouts
1–2 tablespoons dark soy sauce, to taste
1 tablespoon sesame oil
plain/all purpose flour, to assemble
10 spring roll wrappers
vegetable or olive oil, for brushing

ONION RINGS

Onion rings make everything better. Burgers, pizzas, steak, pastas ... just throw an onion ring on top. Made super simply with an air fryer.

1   Bring a small saucepan of salted water to the boil, add the onions and simmer for 5 minutes, until softened. Drain, refresh in cold water and pat dry with kitchen paper.

2   Meanwhile, get the flour, breadcrumbs, paprika, cayenne and a pinch of salt into a shallow bowl. Pour some olive oil into a second bowl.

3   Bathe a few onion rings in the oil, draining off any excess, then toss them in the flour mixture. Repeat with the remaining onion rings.

4   Heat the air fryer to 180°C/350°F.

5   Add the coated onion rings to the air-fryer basket, making sure there is plenty of space between them. Cook for 10–12 minutes, until the rings are crisp and golden. (Do this in batches, depending on the size or your air fryer.) Serve straight away.

MY SUGGESTIONS

Either dip these just as they are (I love them with mayo) or layer them up in your burgers for something extra special.

Serves 4 as a snack

1 large onion, sliced into 1cm/½-inch rings
50g/heaping ⅓ cup plain/all purpose flour
50g/1 cup Panko breadcrumbs
½ teaspoon smoked paprika
¼ teaspoon cayenne pepper, or to taste
pinch of salt
olive oil

CAULIFLOWER CHEESE

A proper good cauliflower cheese can be the make-and-break of a roast dinner. It needs to be saucy. It needs to be thick. It needs to be cheesy. This dish ticks all of those boxes and the air fryer cooks it beautifully.

1   Warm the milk in a saucepan on a low-medium heat, or in a jug in the microwave.

2   In a second small-ish saucepan on a low-medium heat, melt the butter and gradually beat in the flour. You don't want this to start browning, so if you're worried about the temperature, just take it off the heat while you add in the flour to slow things down a little.

3   Once all the flour is in, cook out the flour until the mixture has come to a dough-like consistency and is coming away from the pan (this prevents that tacky, floury texture you can get sometimes with flour in sauces).

4   Little by little, add the warmed milk, making sure you allow each addition to fully incorporate into the sauce before adding more. Keep stirring to avoid lumps (switch to a balloon whisk if you need to).

5   Once you have added all the milk, season the sauce with the salt, pepper, paprika, mustard and nutmeg, then add the cheeses and stir until melted.

6   Heat the air fryer to 170°C/340°F.

7   Put a layer of cauliflower florets in baking tray that fits in your air fryer (fit in what you can and save any left over for another day).

8   Then, pour over the cheese sauce to completely cover, sprinkle over the extra grated cheese and place the tray in the air fryer. Cook for 20 minutes, then turn the heat up to 190°C/375°F and cook for a further 10-15 minutes, until the top is golden and the cauliflower is cooked through.

MY SUGGESTIONS

Serve with your Sunday roast, or as the star of a vegetarian feast!

Serves 4

500ml/2 cups whole milk
50g/3 tablespoons butter
70g/heaping ½ cup plain/all purpose flour
½ teaspoon salt
pinch of ground white pepper
pinch of smoked paprika
1 tablespoon wholegrain mustard
pinch of freshly grated nutmeg
100g/1 cup extra-mature cheddar, grated, plus extra for the top
150g/1½ cups double Gloucester, grated, plus extra for the top
1 cauliflower, broken into similar-sized florets, leaves and all

VEGGIE SAMOSAS

A lovely spice-filled treat that can even replace a sandwich for lunch (make them big!). Filo pastry cooks so well in the air fryer as you know it'll be crispy at the end.

1 Warm the olive oil in a large saucepan over a medium heat. Add the cumin seeds and cook for 30 seconds, until fragrant. Add the onion and ginger and cook for 10 minutes, until the onions are soft and translucent.

2 Stir in the potato and cook with a lid on for 10 minutes, stirring every now and again, until tender. Remove from the heat and add the chilli, garam masala or curry powder, peas, mint and coriander. Stir to combine and season to taste.

3 To assemble the samosas, mix a little flour and water together to make a smooth paste. Lay two sheets of filo pastry on top of one another and cut the sheets into strips, each about 7cm/2¾ inches across.

4 Add a heaped teaspoon of filling at the top of each pastry strip. Place a finger on the top left-hand corner and fold down the top right-hand corner so that you have a diagonal edge. Next, fold the parcel over horizontally, and then diagonally, this time going left to right. Repeat down the length of the pastry and seal the edge with flour-water paste. You should end up with a neat triangle. Repeat with the remaining mixture and filo. Brush the samosas lightly with olive oil.

5 Heat the air fryer to 180°C/350°F.

6 Get the samosas into the air-fryer basket, leaving plenty of space between each (you might need to do this in batches, depending on the size of your air fryer). Cook for 12–14 minutes, until crisp and golden.

MY SUGGESTIONS

Serve with mango chutney, coriander/cilantro chutney, or tamarind chutney for dipping.

Enjoy these as either a side, starter or on a platter with other air-fried treats (the onion bhajis on page 150 are so good with these). You can cook them the day before to take on a picnic for a breadless alternative to a sandwich, if you like.

Makes 20

2 tablespoons olive oil
1 teaspoon cumin seeds
1 onion, finely chopped
3cm/1¼-inch piece fresh ginger, grated or finely chopped (no need to peel)
1 Maris Piper or Russet potato, peeled and cut into 5mm/¼-inch dice
1 red chilli, deseeded and finely chopped
1 teaspoon garam masala or curry powder
200g/heaping 1½ cups frozen peas, defrosted
15g/5 tablespoons mint, leaves finely chopped
15g/5 tablespoons coriander/cilantro, leaves and stems finely chopped
270g/10oz filo pastry
plain/all purpose flour, to assemble

WONTONS

A plate of these beautiful crisp wontons will please any crowd – just make sure you make enough for the people who want one, have two, need three and finish on four.

1 Tip the Chinese leaf lettuce or cabbage into a colander set over a bowl or a sink. Sprinkle over the salt and set aside for 30 minutes.

2 Add the spring onions and ginger to a food processor along with the prawns, pork, soy sauce and sesame oil. Pulse until combined, then squeeze the water out of the cabbage and stir through. Cover and rest in the fridge for at least 30 minutes.

3 To assemble your wontons, place a teaspoon of the filling in the middle of a dumpling wrapper. Use your finger to brush two edges with water and fold the wrapper in half, so that you have a triangle. Press down to squeeze out any air from around the filling. Next, hold the triangle in one hand and use your other hand to draw the two corners together so that they are overlapping, then seal with water. It should look a bit like a boat. You can fold wontons in lots of different ways – this particular shape is called an ingot and is supposed to bring good luck. Place the wonton on a lined baking tray and repeat with the remaining mixture and wrappers.

4 Heat the air fryer to 180°C/350°F.

5 Brush or spray the wontons with a little vegetable oil, and place them in the air-fryer basket, leaving plenty of space between each (do this in batches, depending on the size of your air fryer). Cook for 7–8 minutes, until crisp and golden.

MY SUGGESTIONS

Dig in as they are, fresh out of the air fryer with a side of crispy chilli oil.

Serves 4

½ Chinese leaf lettuce or cabbage (about 230g/3 cups), finely sliced
½ teaspoon salt
3 spring onions, finely sliced
30g/2-inch piece fresh ginger, grated or finely chopped (no need to peel)
165g/6oz raw prawns, peeled, deveined and finely sliced
165g/6oz 10–20% pork mince/ground pork
1 tablespoon dark soy sauce
1 tablespoon sesame oil
20–32 square wonton or dumpling pastry wrappers (defrosted if frozen)
vegetable oil, for brushing or spraying

BLINIS

Blinis is not only a strange word to write out but also an underrated treat. It's essentially a mini pancake to top with cream cheese and smoked fish. A winner at Christmas, but deserving to be appreciated year-round.

1   Sift the flours together into a large bowl, stir in the salt and sprinkle over the yeast.

2   Heat 90ml of the milk and all the soured cream in a small saucepan, until lukewarm.

3   Whisk in the egg yolk, and then gradually whisk the egg mixture into the flour mixture, until you have a smooth batter, adding the remaining milk if necessary. Cover the bowl with a plate or a damp tea towel and leave to rise for about 1 hour.

4   Once the mixture is bubbly, in a separate bowl whisk the egg white to stiff peaks and fold this into the batter.

5   Heat the air fryer to 200°C/400°F and lay a sheet of greaseproof paper in the basket. Working quickly, add teaspoons of mixture to the greaseproof paper, leaving plenty of space between each, and cook for 4–5 minutes, until lightly golden (for optimum deliciousness do this in batches, depending on the size of your air fryer). Then flip the blinis over and cook for another minute. Brush with melted butter and cool on a wire rack.

MY SUGGESTIONS

Serve the blinis warm or at room temperature. To heat them up, wrap them in foil and warm them in the air fryer for a couple of minutes.

Layer your mini pancakes up with cream cheese and your choice of smoked fish to feel extra fancy on a Saturday night.

The blinis here are served with thick crème fraîche, smoked salmon, watercress and lemon, and beetroot hummus, cubed pickled beetroot and smoked mackerel.

Serves 4 (makes a lot!)

45g/⅓ cup strong white bread flour
40g/heaping ¼ cup buckwheat flour
½ teaspoon salt
3.5g/1 teaspoon fast-action yeast
90–100ml/6–7 tablespoons whole milk
75ml/5 tablespoons soured cream
1 egg, separated
30g/2 tablespoons butter, melted

CROQUETAS

Plot twist – an authentic croqueta isn't potato-based. It pains me to leave spuds out of any recipe, but it's worth it when you pull apart that saucy cheesy goodness. No spuds allowed.

1   Melt the butter with a glug of olive oil in a medium saucepan over a medium heat. Add the leek, and about a quarter of the chorizo, and cook for 5–7 minutes, until softened but not coloured. Add 50g/ scant ½ cup of the flour and cook for 8–10 minutes, stirring, until just golden. Remove from the heat and gradually beat in the milk, until you have a smooth sauce. Add the grated cheese, set the pan over a low heat and cook for about 15 minutes, until thickened. It should be the consistency of smooth mashed potato.

2   Add the remaining chorizo, season to taste with salt, some grated nutmeg and lots of black pepper (it should be really peppery). Leave the mixture to cool, then cover the surface of the sauce with cling film to stop a skin forming, and refrigerate it for at least 2 hours.

3   When you're ready to cook, take heaped teaspoonfuls of the sauce mixture and roll each one into a neat ball. Place the balls on a lined baking tray. (You should have enough mixture for 16 balls altogether.)

4   Heat the air fryer to 220°C/425°F (or your air fryer's maximum temperature).

5   Find three shallow bowls. Crack the eggs into one and whisk gently. Add the remaining flour to the second bowl and the breadcrumbs to the third. Lightly season the breadcrumbs.

6   Using one hand for the wet ingredients (eggs) and the other for the dry ingredients (flour and breadcrumbs), toss a ball of sauce mixture in the flour, then the egg, then the breadcrumbs. Repeat the process for a second time to fully coat, and place the balls back on the baking tray. Repeat with the remaining balls.

7   Lightly drizzle the croquetas in olive oil and roll them around until evenly coated. Place them in the air-fryer basket, leaving plenty of space between each one (you might have to do this in batches, depending on the size of your air fryer). Cook for 8–10 minutes, until crisp and golden.

MY SUGGESTIONS

Add a twist with some finely chopped Spanish ham in the cheese filling, or even chopped ham hock.

Makes 16

50g/3 tablespoons butter
olive oil
1 small leek, finely chopped
80g/3oz chorizo, finely chopped
90g/¾ cup plain/all purpose flour
400ml/1⅔ cups whole milk
80g/heaping ¾ cup manchego, grated
freshly grated nutmeg, to taste
2 eggs
100g/2 cups Panko breadcrumbs
salt and ground black pepper

MOZZARELLA DIPPERS

Let it be known, starters are my favourite course of the meal. Fun fact: I'm a bit of a super-fan of an American-style diner restaurant which may or may not sound similar to TGI-Thursdays (I'd literally have every single one of my birthday parties there). As a family we'd always order a load of starters instead of mains – and mozzarella dippers were a must on the table.

1   Pat the mozzarella dry with kitchen paper, cut it into quarters, then cut each quarter lengthways into four, so that you end up with 16 long sticks of mozzarella.

2   Heat the air fryer to 220°C/425°F (or your air fryer's maximum temperature).

3   Find three shallow bowls. Crack the eggs into one and whisk gently. Add the flour to the second bowl and the breadcrumbs, oregano, garlic powder and onion powder to the third. Generously season the breadcrumb mixture.

4   Using one hand for the wet ingredients (eggs) and the other for the dry ingredients (flour and breadcrumbs), toss a piece of mozzarella in the flour, then the egg, then the breadcrumbs. Repeat the process for a second time, to coat fully, and place the mozzarella stick on a lined baking tray. Repeat with the remaining mozzarella sticks.

5   Lightly drizzle or spray the mozzarella sticks with olive oil and get them in the air-fryer basket, leaving plenty of space between each one (do this in batches, depending on the size of your air fryer). Cook for 5–7 minutes, until crisp and golden.

Makes 16

400g/14oz block of
   cooking mozzarella
   (mozzarella cucina)
4 eggs
50g/heaping ⅓ cup
   plain/all purpose flour
120g/2¼ cups Panko
   breadcrumbs
1 teaspoon dried
   oregano
1 teaspoon garlic
   powder
1 teaspoon onion
   powder
olive oil, for drizzling
   or spraying
sea-salt flakes and
   black pepper

MY SUGGESTIONS

Mozzarella string cheese would be perfect for this.

This is another great little starter item that would go with a selection of other bits in this book – trust me, you have the means right here to offer your guests the ultimate platter to kick off dinner.

GARLIC BREAD

I love to make garlic bread in the air fryer – lay it out on the table, lashings of sea salt, and just CRUNCH down with a knife along the crispy crunchy deliciousness. Serve as a side, starter or snack whenever the occasion calls for it.

1   Cream the butter with a fork, until pale, then add the garlic and parsley and mix until smooth. You might find this easier to do in a food processor. Season to taste with salt and pepper.

2   Cut slices along the length of the baguette, cutting only about two-thirds of the way through the loaf so as not to slice it completely, and spread the garlic butter evenly into the gaps. Don't hold back.

3   Heat the air fryer to 200°C/400°F.

4   Wrap the filled baguette with foil, place it in the air-fryer basket and cook for 15 minutes, until warmed through and the garlicky butter is melted and oozy. (You can cut the baguette into sections to fit the air-fryer basket if you need to.)

MY SUGGESTIONS

You know what to do with a delicious loaf of garlic bread – whether it's on the side of pasta, meat or a chilli con carne, it's time to tear, share and enjoy!

Use roasted garlic or confit garlic (see page 100) for a deep, caramelised flavour, if you prefer.

You could add thyme, chilli or Parmesan (or almost anything) to the butter for different flavour combos.

Depending on the size of your baguette, you may have some leftover garlic butter to freeze or keep in the fridge and use for the garlic mushrooms on page 146.

Serves 4

150g/½ cup plus 2 tablespoons butter, softened
6 garlic cloves, crushed
15g/5 tablespoons flat-leaf parsley, finely chopped
1 crusty baguette, artisan or cheap and cheerful
sea-salt flakes and black pepper

MAC AND CHEESE

Oven-baked pasta dishes add that deliciously melted cheesiness throughout with a crusty top for a bit of texture. But why not do that bit in the air fryer from now on? It speeds up the process and the results are just as good.

1   Warm the milk in a saucepan on a low–medium heat, or in a jug in the microwave.

2   In a second small-ish saucepan on a low–medium heat, melt the butter and gradually beat in the flour. You don't want this to start browning, so if you're worried about the temperature, just take it off the heat while you add in the flour to slow things down a little.

3   Cook out the flour until the mixture has come to a dough-like consistency and is coming away from the pan (this prevents that tacky, floury texture you can get sometimes with flour in sauces).

4   Little by little, add the warmed milk, making sure you allow each addition to fully incorporate into the sauce before adding more. Keep stirring to avoid lumps (switch to a balloon whisk if you need to) and cook over a medium heat for 3 minutes to get it all lovely and thick. Add the grated cheddar and double Gloucester, season with the nutmeg, white pepper and salt and set aside.

5   Tip the macaroni into a pan of boiling salted water, stirring a couple of times to prevent it all sticking together, and leave it to cook for 8 minutes, until it's al dente. You don't want to cook it all the way as it will carry on cooking in the oven.

6   Heat the air fryer to 180°C/350°F.

7   Drain the pasta and add it to the pan with the sauce, stirring to coat it completely. Pour a layer of the cheesy mac into a baking dish that fits in your air fryer, not filling all the way, then tear up the mozzarella ball and add this on top. Pour the rest of the cheesy mac over the top.

8   Sprinkle over the breadcrumbs and Parmesan and then get it into the air fryer 15–20 minutes to turn golden, gooey and crunchy.

MY SUGGESTIONS

Serve this either as a main dish, as a side with something delicious like some of the air-fried breaded chicken (see page 27), or ... have you ever tried mac and cheese alongside a roast dinner? A wonder from across the Pond and, trust me, it's actually delicious!

Serves 4

50g/3 tablespoons butter
70g/heaping ½ cup plain/all purpose flour
500ml/2 cups whole milk
100g/1 cup extra-mature cheddar, grated
150g/1½ cups double Gloucester, grated
pinch of freshly grated nutmeg
pinch of ground white pepper
½ teaspoon salt
300g/10oz dried macaroni
1 x 125g/5oz ball of mozzarella
50g/1 cup Panko breadcrumbs
90g/scant 1 cup Parmesan, grated

SWEET TREATS

BLUEBERRY MUFFINS

A lovely little recipe that one day I hope will serve me well as a grandma, who'll cook them and leave them on the kitchen worktop for the grandchildren to smell and run to after a long day of picking daisies in the garden. Nah. If it's me, Grandma will have finished them all and the kids can have a Snickers instead. Sorry.

1   Heat the air fryer to 160°C/325°F. Line a muffin tray with muffin cases or see notes below for an alternative.

2   In a large bowl, whisk together the flour, baking powder and salt.

3   In a separate bowl, whisk together the eggs and sugar until thick and pale (about 4–5 minutes). Add the buttermilk, lemon zest and oil and whisk briefly, until just combined. Fold the dry ingredients through the wet ingredients, then gently fold through the diced apple and the blueberries, holding back a few blueberries for the topping.

4   Divide the mixture between the muffin cases and scatter over the remaining blueberries and some demerara sugar.

5   Place the muffin tray in the air-fryer basket and bake for 18–20 minutes, or until a skewer inserted into the centre of a muffin comes out clean. Allow to cool in the tray, before placing on a wire rack and cooling fully.

MY SUGGESTIONS

Serve up on a plate, freshly baked, and the rest is magic!

The type of muffin tray you need depends on the size of your air fryer (if a 6-cup muffin tray fits, use this and bake in two batches), or you can make a rough-and-ready muffin mould out of foil to support the cases.

Makes 12

200g/1⅔ cups plain/ all purpose flour (or 150g/1 cup plus 2 tablespoons plain/ all purpose flour and 50g/½ cup plus 1 tablespoon wholemeal flour), sifted
2 teaspoons baking powder
pinch of salt
2 eggs
150g/¾ cup light brown soft sugar
200ml/¾ cup plus 1 tablespoon buttermilk (shop bought is best)
1 lemon, zested
100ml/7 tablespoons vegetable oil
1 small, tart apple, peeled, cored and cut into 5mm/¼-inch dice
200g/1½ cups blueberries (frozen is fine)
1–2 tablespoons demerara sugar, for sprinkling

STRAWBERRY CHEESECAKE MUFFINS

A cheesecake muffin is a hybrid I can get behind. Naughtily sweet cream cheese and strawberry cutting through your classically baked muffin. It blows my mind how good bakes are in the air fryer.

1 First, make the streusel topping by rubbing together the flour and butter between your fingers until the mixture resembles breadcrumbs. Use a pestle to crush the cardamom seeds in a mortar, then add the crushed seeds to the butter mixture along with the sugar and cinnamon. Transfer the mixture to the fridge while you make the muffins.

2 Heat the air fryer to 180°C/350°F. Line a muffin tray with muffin cases, or see notes below for an alternative.

3 Make the muffins. Sift the flours into a bowl, add the baking powder and salt, and stir to combine.

4 In another large bowl, whisk the eggs and sugar together until thick and pale (about 4–5 minutes). Add the cream cheese, milk, vanilla and oil and whisk briefly, until just combined. Fold through the dry ingredients, then gently fold through the strawberries.

5 Divide the mixture equally between the muffin cases and scatter over the streusel topping.

6 Put the muffin tray into the air-fryer basket and bake for 18–22 minutes, or until a skewer inserted into the centre of a muffin comes out clean. Allow the muffins to cool in the tray, then transfer them to a wire rack to cool fully before scoffing.

MY SUGGESTIONS

Perfect for the bake sale or picnic. Serve them warm for that extra baked freshness.

The type of muffin tray you need depends on the size of your air fryer (if a 6-cup muffin tray fits, use this and bake in two batches), or you can make a rough-and-ready muffin mould out of foil to support the cases.

Makes 12

150g/1 cup plus 2 tablespoons plain/all purpose flour
50g/½ cup plus 1 tablespoon wholemeal flour
2 teaspoons baking powder
pinch of salt
2 eggs
150g/¾ cup light brown soft sugar
100g/7 tablespoons full-fat cream cheese
50ml/3 tablespoons plus 1 teaspoon whole milk
½ teaspoon vanilla paste
100ml/7 tablespoons vegetable oil
200g/1½ cups strawberries, roughly chopped

For the streusel topping

75g/⅔ cups plain/all purpose flour, sifted
50g/3 tablespoons plus 1 teaspoon unsalted butter, diced
4 cardamom pods, seeds removed (shells discarded)
35g/3 tablespoons demerara sugar
pinch of ground cinnamon

CHOCOLATE MUFFINS

This air-fryer muffin recipe is exactly the thing you need if you want to mix up some sweet goodies in no time at all. There's only one thing better than cakes, and that's quick cakes. The quicker they go from raw egg to my mouth, the better.

1 Heat the air fryer to 160°C/325°F. Line a muffin tray with muffin cases, or see notes below for an alternative.

2 In a large bowl, whisk together the flour, baking powder, cocoa powder and coffee powder. Set aside a few oats to sprinkle, then add the rest to the bowl.

3 In a separate bowl, whisk together the eggs and sugar until thick and pale (about 4–5 minutes). Add the buttermilk, vanilla and oil and whisk briefly, until just combined. Fold the dry ingredients through the wet ingredients, then gently fold through 100g/½ cup of the chopped chocolate.

4 Divide the mixture equally between the muffin cases and scatter over the remaining chocolate and oats, the demerara sugar and sea-salt flakes.

5 Place the muffin tray in the air-fryer basket and bake for 18–20 minutes, or until a skewer inserted into the centre of a muffin comes out clean. Allow to cool in the tray, before placing on a wire rack and cooling fully.

MY SUGGESTIONS

The type of muffin tray you need depends on the size of your air fryer (if a 6-cup muffin tray fits, use this and bake in two batches), or you can make a rough-and-ready muffin mould out of foil to support the cases.

Makes 12

200g/1⅔ cups plain/all purpose flour, sifted
2 teaspoons baking powder
30g/⅓ cup cocoa powder
1 teaspoon instant coffee powder
30g/⅓ cup jumbo oats
2 eggs
150g/¾ cups light brown soft sugar
200ml/¾ cup plus 1 tablespoon buttermilk (shop bought is best)
½ teaspoon vanilla paste
100ml/7 tablespoons vegetable oil
150g/¾ cup 70% dark chocolate, roughly chopped
2 tablespoons demerara sugar
pinch of sea-salt flakes

SPICED DONUT HOLES

A donut hole is quite simply ... the hole of the donut (or, I suppose, the bit taken out to make the hole). It's kind of like your sweet version of a savoury dough ball. Little balls of sugary donuts. Douse in sugar and eat them warm to feel like you're at a fairground on bonfire night.

1   Put the butter and milk in a microwaveable bowl and blast on high power for a few seconds until just melted and a bit warm. Remove from the microwave, add the yeast and egg and mix well.

2   Put the flour, sugar and ground spices in a large bowl or the bowl of a stand mixer, and add the wet mixture. Beat (using the beater attachment in a mixer or a wooden spoon by hand) for a good 5–10 minutes, until fully combined and smooth.

3   Cover the bowl with a tea towel and leave the mixture to prove in a warm spot for an hour or so, or until it's doubled in size.

4   On a flour-dusted surface, roll out the dough until it is an even 1cm/½-inch thickness.

5   Use a round, 2.5cm/1-inch cutter to cut out as many circles as you can from the dough. You can re-roll the trimmings once to cut some more (but only once). Place the dough circles on a sheet of greaseproof paper.

6   Heat the air fryer to 180°C/350°F. Make the coating: combine the sugar and spices in a mixing bowl and set aside for later.

7   Spray the air-fryer basket with vegetable oil and put the dough circles inside, leaving plenty of space between each (you may have to do this in batches, depending on the size of your air fryer). Cook for 3 minutes, until golden, then repeat for the other batches if necessary. Toss each batch in the flavoured sugar while hot and dig in.

MY SUGGESTIONS

To make a caramel sauce for dipping, add 150g of caster/superfine sugar to a heavy-based deep pan and set over a medium–high heat to melt. In a separate pan, warm 100ml of double/heavy cream with a deseeded vanilla pod (reserve the seeds). Once the sugar is a light golden colour, carefully and slowly whisk in the warmed cream until combined then remove from the heat. Bit by bit, whisk in 70g of salted butter and the vanilla seeds, until well mixed and smooth.

Serves 6–8

40g/2 tablespoons plus 2 teaspoons unsalted butter
100ml/7 tablespoons whole milk
1 x 7g/¼oz sachet of fast-action yeast
1 egg
280g/2¼ cups plain/all purpose flour, plus extra for dusting
50g/¼ cup caster/superfine sugar
1 teaspoon ground cinnamon
pinch of ground cloves
pinch of freshly grated nutmeg
vegetable oil, for spraying

For the sugar coating

100g/½ cup caster/superfine sugar
10g/scant 2 teaspoons ground cinnamon
pinch of freshly grated nutmeg
pinch of ground cloves

SLUTTY BROWNIES

Now don't be shocked by the name, but there's no other word to describe how
deliciously naughty, decadent and in some ways X-rated these brownies are. Layers
of cookie, Oreos AND brownies. I'm willing to be extra-naughty for these.

1   Line an ovenproof dish that fits in your air fryer with greaseproof
    paper (the one used in this recipe is 21 x 15cm/8½ x 6 inches).

2   For the cookie base, beat the butter and sugar until light and fluffy.
    Beat in the egg and then sift in the flour, bicarbonate of soda
    and cornflour. Mix together to form a dough and crumble in the
    chocolate.

3   Transfer this dough to your ovenproof dish, forming a flat layer
    which comes around a third of the way up your dish, and leave in
    the fridge for at least for 10 minutes. You might have leftover cookie
    dough but you can keep this and freeze it for another time, or for
    emergency cookies.

4   Meanwhile, make the brownie layer. Put the chocolate and butter in
    a microwaveable bowl and heat in the microwave until just melted.
    Leave to cool to room temperature.

5   Whisk together the eggs and sugar, until very fluffy and pale, then
    fold in the chocolate and butter. Sift in the cocoa powder and flour
    and fold in, then fold in the chocolate chunks.

6   Heat the air fryer to 160°C/325°F.

7   Remove the ovenproof dish from the fridge and add a layer of Oreo
    biscuits on top of the layer of cookie dough, pressing them in firmly.
    Pour the brownie mixture over the top to fill the container.

8   Transfer the dish to the air-fryer basket and bake for 25–30 minutes,
    until the brownie layer has that lovely cracked look on top.

9   Remove the dish from the air fryer and leave the brownies to cool in
    the dish for 20 minutes. Remove from the dish and cut into squares
    to serve.

MY SUGGESTIONS

Try using different biscuits as the middle layer. Biscoffs (and some
spread), custard creams or chocolate Bourbons are all good options.

Makes 9

For the cookie base
115g/½ cup unsalted
    butter, softened
125g/⅔ cup light brown
    soft sugar
1 egg
225g/1¾ cups plus 1
    tablespoon plain/all
    purpose flour
½ teaspoon bicarbonate
    of soda/baking soda
1 tablespoon cornflour/
    cornstarch
200g/1 cup plus 2
    tablespoons milk
    chocolate, roughly
    chopped

For the brownie layer
3 eggs
200g/1 cup caster/
    superfine sugar
200g/7oz 70% dark
    chocolate, broken into
    pieces
200g/¾ cup plus 1
    tablespoon butter
75g/¾ cup cocoa
    powder
100g/¾ cup plus 1
    tablespoon plain/all
    purpose flour
50g/½ cup white
    chocolate, cut into
    large chunks
50g/½ cup milk
    chocolate, cut into
    large chunks
1 packet of Oreo biscuits

PECAN AND PRETZEL BLONDIES

Like a brownie but more biscuity with white chocolate, vanilla and nuts. I couldn't tell you which is better so you're going to have to try these and my slutty brownies (see page 180) and brownies (see page 184) and let me know which you prefer.

1 Line a 20 x 20cm/8 x 8 inch baking tin or one that will fit in your air fryer (as long as the depth of the batter is roughly the same, it won't make too much difference to the cooking time).

2 Melt the butter in a saucepan over a medium-high heat and let it bubble vigorously for 4–5 minutes. Brown speckles will appear in the foamy amber butter and it should smell nutty. Watch the butter carefully as it has a habit of bubbling over. Remove from the heat and leave to cool for about 15 minutes.

3 Heat the air fryer to 150°C/300°F.

4 In a large bowl or stand mixer, whisk together the eggs and sugar until thick and pale. With the mixer running, pour in the browned butter, then add the vanilla paste. Fold in the flour and sea-salt flakes. Set aside some of the chocolate, pecans and pretzels for sprinkling, then fold the rest through until just combined.

5 Tip the mixture into the tin and smooth into an even layer. Scatter over the remaining chocolate, pecans and pretzels and the pinch of sea-salt flakes.

6 Place the tin in the air-fryer basket and bake the blondies for 20–25 minutes, or until just set. Remove from the oven and leave to cool completely before slicing. For extra deliciousness, place the blondies in the fridge overnight before eating.

Makes 16

200g/¾ cup plus 1 tablespoon unsalted butter, cubed
3 eggs
200g/1 cup light brown soft sugar
½ teaspoon vanilla paste
100g/¾ cup plus 1 tablespoon plain/all purpose flour, sifted
1 teaspoon sea-salt flakes, plus a pinch for the top
200g/1 cup plus 2 tablespoons milk chocolate, roughly chopped
100g/heaping ¾ cup pecans, toasted and roughly chopped
100g/heaping ¾ cup salted pretzels

MY SUGGESTIONS

So many options for mixing these up. For dark chocolate and stem ginger: add 200g/1 cup plus 2 tablespoons of roughly chopped 70% dark chocolate and 50g/¼ cup of roughly chopped stem ginger.

For milk chocolate, sesame and pretzel: add 200g/1 cup plus 2 tablespoons of roughly chopped milk chocolate, 2 tablespoons of tahini and 50g/¾ cup of broken-up hard salted or sesame pretzels.

Some of my other flavour combos are cherry and almond or lemon zest and dark chocolate.

BROWNIES

These are my ultimate brownies and are beautiful warm or cold, but my favourite way to serve them is extra-warm with a good ol' dollop of ice cream on top. Delicious!

1 Melt the butter and dark chocolate together in a microwaveable bowl in short bursts on full power in the microwave, or in a heatproof bowl set over a pan of gently simmering water.

2 Meanwhile, in a stand mixer fitted with the whisk attachment, or using a hand whisk, whisk the eggs and sugar together until light and fluffy.

3 Sift together the cocoa powder and flour and leave to the side until needed.

4 Heat the air fryer to 150°C/300°F.

5 Once the chocolate and butter mixture is fully melted and cooled to room temperature and the eggs are fluffy, start folding the chocolate mixture into the egg mixture until fully combined.

6 Then, in three parts, fold in the flour until evenly distributed.

7 Line a baking tray that is the right size to fit inside your air fryer with greaseproof paper and fill it with the brownie mixture (if you have any brownie mixture left over because of the size of the tin that will fit, it's not a problem – if you have enough for a small, second batch, use it in the slutty brownies on page 180 – extra brownie mixture is never anything to complain about).

8 Place the baking tray in the air fryer and bake for 25 minutes, until crackled on top and gooey in the middle. Leave the brownie in the tin to cool a little, then score the mixture and cut it into squares. Eat warm or cold.

MY SUGGESTIONS

Try adding different kinds of chocolate to the mixture: a combo of dark, milk and white for a full-on chocolate trio brownie is unbeatable. Or, pour the batter into the tin half at a time, adding a layer of caramel sauce in the middle for some real luxury.

Makes 16

200g/¾ cup plus 1 tablespoon salted butter
200g/7oz 70% dark chocolate
3 eggs
200g/1 cup caster/ superfine sugar
75g/¾ cup cocoa powder
100g/¾ cup plus 1 tablespoon plain/all purpose flour

ROASTED RUM-GLAZED PINEAPPLE

It's time to get a bit fruity now! There's always a big debate on whether hot fruit works and I think a roasted pineapple makes the answer easy. Fruity, sweet and hearty, with a rum glaze, this hot fruit dish is as warming as it is surprisingly refreshing.

1 Make a glaze. Add everything except the pineapple to a saucepan and bring to the boil, then turn the heat down to medium and cook until you have a glaze consistency. This should take around 5–10 minutes – just keep an eye on it so it doesn't burn. Remove from the heat and leave to one side for later.

2 Heat the air fryer to 180°C/350°F.

3 Get the pineapple sticks or wedges into the air-fryer basket for 5 minutes. Then, using a brush, glaze them up with your rum glaze, give them a turn and return them back to the air fryer for a further 5 minutes. Re-glaze and repeat one more time, until you have beautifully golden, glazed, sticky, sweet pineapple sticks. Serve hot and juicy!

MY SUGGESTIONS

To serve, get some coconut ice cream on the side and a little lime zest grated over the top. Just perfect for a summer day.

Serves 4

50g/¼ cup dark brown soft sugar
2 tablespoons water
3 tablespoons spiced rum
pinch of ground cinnamon
pinch of freshly grated nutmeg
1 lime, zested and juiced
1 pineapple, peeled, cored and cut into wedges or sticks

FLAPJACKS

A quick and easy snack that's perfect for breakfast, lunchboxes, on-the-go or sat
at home. Mix up with different flavours based on your tastes.

1   Heat the air fryer to 150°C/300°F. Line a small baking tin (about 20 x
    30cm/8 x 12 inches) that will fit in your air fryer.

2   Melt the butter, sugar and golden syrup in a saucepan. Add the oats
    and pinch of salt, and stir to combine. Tip the mixture into the tin and
    press it into the corners. It doesn't need to be completely smooth as
    any lumps and bumps will become deliciously crunchy.

3   Place the tin in the air-fryer basket and bake the flapjacks for 18–20
    minutes, until golden all over. Leave to cool in the tin, before turning
    out onto a wire rack and cooling completely. Once cool, slice into
    squares. You might find it easier to score the squares before the
    flapjack is completely cool.

MY SUGGESTIONS

These are perfect as they are. Or, try them warm with some
delicious custard for a Sunday roast dessert.

This is a simple, classic recipe and it's so easy to change up the
flavourings: try nuts, seeds, dried fruit, peanut butter, almond butter,
lemon zest, orange zest, chocolate or anything you fancy.

If you're using a much smaller baking tin to fit your air fryer, increase
the cooking time slightly to allow for a deeper mixture, and check
the flapjack frequently.

Makes 12

*150g/½ cup plus 2
    tablespoons unsalted
    butter*
*150g/¾ cup light brown
    soft sugar*
*2 tablespoons golden
    syrup*
*250g/2½ cups oats (I
    like half jumbo oats
    and half rolled)*
pinch of sea-salt flakes

BAKED CHEESECAKE

Again with the shock, but ... cheesecake? In an air fryer? Take a step back, compose yourself, and then go make this DELICIOUS dessert. I'm actually going to go make it right now.

1   Heat the air fryer to 140°C/285°F. Line the base of a 20cm/8-inch springform tin with greaseproof paper, or use whatever size springform tin fits in your air fryer. You might like to wrap the base and sides of the tin with foil to prevent any leakages.

2   Blitz the biscuits in a food processor until fine. Melt the butter in a small saucepan and stir in the crushed biscuits. Press the mixture evenly into the bottom of the tin and place in the fridge for about 30 minutes, until firm.

3   In a large bowl, beat the cream cheese, soured cream, eggs, egg yolk, sugar, lemon zest and vanilla until combined. Fold in the cornflour.

4   Pour the mixture into the tin and smooth it out evenly. Carefully place the tin in the air-fryer basket and bake the cheesecake for 45–60 minutes, until just set (but decrease the cooking time if you're using a smaller tin). Turn off the air fryer, open the drawer a little and leave the cheesecake to cool before removing. Once cool, chill in the fridge (overnight if you can wait that long) before serving.

Serves 8

250g/9oz digestive biscuits
75g/5 tablespoons unsalted butter
600g/2½ cups full-fat cream cheese
300g/1¼ cups soured cream
3 whole eggs, plus 1 yolk
250g/1¼ cups golden caster/superfine sugar
1 lemon, zested
½ teaspoon vanilla paste
3 tablespoons cornflour/ cornstarch

MY SUGGESTIONS

Slice this up and enjoy it on its own or with a super-quick berry compote: heat up 300g/2⅓ cups of mixed frozen berries in a saucepan, add 3 tablespoons of icing sugar and a drop of vanilla extract, and cook on a medium heat until thickened and sweet. Easy.

If you can't find digestive biscuits, use graham crackers instead.

BASQUE CHEESECAKE

Very fancy, very continental, and very EASY in the air fryer. A Basque cheesecake has a gorgeous, almost burnt top that gives a slightly bitter edge that has to be tried to be believed for its deliciousness. Enjoy – and feel fancy.

1 Heat the air fryer to 200°C/400°F. Line a 20cm/8-inch springform tin with greaseproof paper, or use whatever size springform tin fits in your air fryer. The paper needs to come above the sides of the tin, making sure that there are no gaps.

2 In a large bowl, beat the cream cheese and sugar until smooth. Add the lemon zest and vanilla and briefly combine.

3 Beat in the eggs one at a time, then the egg yolk, followed by the double cream and soured cream. Fold in the cornflour and sea-salt flakes. Pour the mixture into the prepared tin.

4 Place the tin in the air-fryer basket and bake the cheesecake for 45–50 minutes, until dark brown (it will need less time if you're using a smaller tin). The cheesecake should be cracked around the edges, but still wobbly in the middle. Remove from the air fryer and leave to cool in the tin (overnight if you can wait that long) before serving.

MY SUGGESTIONS

Ready to go, so just dig in and enjoy!

Serves 8

650g/2¾ cups full-fat cream cheese
250g/1¼ cups golden caster/superfine sugar
1 lemon, zested
½ teaspoon vanilla paste
4 whole eggs, plus 1 yolk
230ml/scant 1 cup double/heavy cream
150ml/⅔ cup soured cream
35g/2 tablespoons plus 2 teaspoons cornflour/cornstarch
pinch of sea-salt flakes

CLASSIC COOKIES

Cookies are great, and I genuinely think they're at their best when they've just been baked – a little bit warm and a little bit melty – and the air fryer is the perfect way to get this in the quickest time. I love this recipe because you probably have the ingredients in the cupboard and you could have some warm cookies in no time.

1   Line a baking tray with greaseproof paper. Using a stand mixer fitted with the paddle attachment, or a hand whisk, combine the butter and sugar together until light and fluffy with no crunchy bits left.

2   Whisk in the egg, then sift in the flour, bicarbonate of soda and cornflour, to form a dough. Break off pieces of dough, each about 50g/3 tablespoons, and roll them into little balls. Roll the balls in the chopped chocolate and place them on the lined baking tray. Transfer to the fridge and chill the cookies for at least 10 minutes to firm up.

3   Heat the air fryer to 160°C/325°F and line the air-fryer basket with greaseproof paper.

4   Gently flatten the balls slightly and place them in the air fryer to cook for 12 minutes, making sure they're spaced well apart. How many you can cook at one time will depend on the size of your air fryer.

5   Once they are cooked, remove from the air fryer and leave to cool for, like, 1 minute before digging in. Repeat for the next batch.

Makes 12

115g/½ cup unsalted butter
125g/⅔ cup light brown soft sugar
1 egg
225g/1¾ cups plus 1 tablespoon plain/all purpose flour
½ teaspoon bicarbonate of soda/baking soda
1 tablespoon cornflour/ cornstarch
200–300g/ 1 cup plus 2 tablespoons–2 cups milk chocolate, roughly chopped

MY SUGGESTIONS

For vegan cookies, mix 60ml/¼ cup of vegetable oil, a dash of vanilla extract, 50g/¼ cup of light brown soft sugar, 50g/¼ cup of caster/ superfine sugar and 35ml/2 tablespoons plus 2 teaspoons of water in a bowl. Sift in 150g/1 cup plus 2 tablespoons of plain/all purpose flour, and a pinch each of bicarbonate of soda and baking powder. Follow the recipe as above, using 200g/1 cup plus 1 tablespoons of vegan dark chocolate to roll the balls in.

To make stuffed cookies, take 1 teaspoon of, let's say, hazelnut spread, and put it on a piece of greaseproof paper on a baking tray. Keep going until you have as many teaspoons as you want stuffed cookies. Pop the tray in the freezer and leave the little mounds to freeze. When you make your cookie dough, take 50g/3 tablespoons, flatten it out, and add a frozen teaspoon of spread. Mould another piece of cookie dough over the top, pinching the dough together to make sure the spread is fully encased. Repeat, refrigerate the cookies for 30 minutes and then air-fry as in the recipe above.

CUPCAKES

A great recipe to cook with kids, or to cook as a hungry 29-year-old chef who's still a big kid at heart. Lots of sprinkles please.

1   Heat the air fryer to 160°C/325°F. Line a cupcake tin with cupcake cases, or see notes below for an alternative.

2   Cream the butter and sugar together until light and fluffy. Add the eggs one at a time, adding a spoonful of flour each time, followed by the vanilla. Fold in the remaining flour and the salt. Divide the mixture equally between the cupcake cases.

3   Place the cupcake tin in the air-fryer basket and bake the cupcakes for 20–25 minutes, or until a skewer inserted into the centres comes out clean. Allow the cupcakes to cool in the tray, before placing on a wire rack to cool fully.

4   To make the icing, gradually add the lemon juice to the icing sugar and mix until smooth. Spoon over the cupcakes and sprinkle with the sugar sprinkles. Voilà!

MY SUGGESTIONS

You know what to do with these: decorate as you fancy and put on a big plate for everyone to enjoy.

You could swap the sprinkles for rose petals, edible flowers or chocolate sprinkles.

The cupcake tin depends on the size of your air fryer (if a 6-cup cupcake tin fits, use this and bake in two batches), or you can make a rough-and-ready cupcake mould out of foil to support the cases.

Makes 12

3 eggs, weighed (you need to know for the other ingredients; about 175–180g/¾ cup)
same weight/¾ cup of unsalted butter
same weight/¾ cup plus 2 tablespoons of light brown soft sugar
same weight/1⅓ cups plus 1 tablespoon of self-raising flour
¼ teaspoon vanilla paste
pinch of salt

For the icing
1½ tablespoons lemon juice
150g/1½ cups icing sugar, sifted
sugar sprinkles

CHOCOLATE FUDGE CAKES

Live your full Bruce Bogtrotter fantasies with these delicious chocolate fudge cakes.
If you're like me and saw that scene from Matilda as less of a punishment, more of a
dream-come-true, make these cakes and shove them in your mouth!

1 Heat the air fryer to 160°C/325°F. Line a cupcake or muffin tray with
   cupcake cases, or see notes below for an alternative.

2 Melt the dark chocolate and butter together in a heatproof bowl set
   over a pan of gently simmering water or in a microwave. Stir briefly
   to combine, then remove from the heat.

3 Meanwhile, add the flour, baking powder, bicarbonate of soda, sugar,
   cocoa powder and salt to a large bowl and whisk together.

4 Whisk the eggs, buttermilk and coffee into the chocolate mixture
   until evenly combined, then fold in the dry ingredients.

5 Spoon the mixture equally into the cupcake cases and bake for 18–20
   minutes (on or off the baking tray, depending on the size of your air-
   fryer basket; see notes), or until a skewer inserted into the centre of
   the cupcakes comes out clean. Remove from the air fryer and allow
   to cool in the tray, before placing on a wire rack and cooling fully.

6 To make the ganache, add the chocolates, golden syrup and sea-salt
   flakes to a heatproof bowl. Warm the cream in a small saucepan
   until steaming, then pour the hot cream over the chocolate mixture
   and whisk to combine. Allow to cool for 10 minutes or so, so that it's
   spreadable but not runny.

7 Spoon the ganache on top of the cakes and allow to set before
   serving.

MY SUGGESTIONS

I like these with a glass of cold milk – childish, I know, but delicious.
Cakes and muffins are also best enjoyed with friends so, get the
kettle on, get the air fryer plugged in, invite the neighbour over and
have a lovely chinwag.

The cupcake tin depends on the size of your air fryer (if a 6-cup
muffin tin fits, use this and bake in two batches), or you can make a
rough-and-ready cupcake mould out of foil to support the cases.

Makes 12

*200g/7oz 70% dark
   chocolate, broken into
   pieces*
*200g/¾ cup plus 1
   tablespoon unsalted
   butter*
*1¼ cups plus 2
   tablespoons plain/all
   purpose flour, sifted*
*1 teaspoon baking
   powder*
*1 teaspoon bicarbonate
   of soda/baking soda*
*200g/1 cup light brown
   soft sugar*
*60g/¾ cup cocoa
   powder, sifted*
pinch of salt
3 eggs
*100ml/7 tablespoons
   buttermilk (shop
   bought is best)*
*55ml/4 tablespoons
   espresso coffee*

**For the chocolate
   ganache**
*50g/2oz 70% dark
   chocolate, broken
   into pieces*
*50g/2oz milk chocolate,
   broken into pieces*
*1 tablespoon golden
   syrup*
pinch of sea-salt flakes
*100ml/7 tablespoons
   double/heavy cream*

FRENCH TOAST BITES

Another dipping favourite of mine – and surprisingly easy to whip up for a treat breakfast, snack or dessert. (I've noticed writing this book that I could eat almost ANYTHING as just a 'quick snack' and honestly the air fryer has made it even more possible.)

Serves 4

1   Melt the butter in a small pan over a low heat or in a microwave, and pour it into a shallow dish. Whisk in the milk, eggs, lemon zest, vanilla seeds and pod, cinnamon and salt.

2   Cut each slice of bread into bite-sized pieces and press each one into the egg mixture. Leave to soak for 10 minutes.

3   Heat the air fryer to 180°C/350°F. Add the pieces of bread to the air-fryer basket, leaving plenty of space between them, and cook for 8–10 minutes, until golden.

MY SUGGESTIONS

Serve with fresh fruit or a chocolate dipping sauce, or even warm hazelnut spread for extra ease.

For extra decadence, you could swap bread for brioche, croissant or pain au chocolat.

100g/7 tablespoons butter
160ml/⅔ cup whole milk
2 eggs
½ lemon, zested
¼ teaspoon vanilla paste, or 1 vanilla pod, seeds scraped out
generous pinch of ground cinnamon
pinch of salt
4 thick slices of bread
icing sugar, for dusting

CHURROS WITH CHILLI CHOCOLATE DIPPING SAUCE

Is there a more beautiful sight than a big, long, thick churro being dunked into decadent, deep, saucy chocolate? I need a moment on that thought.

1 To make the churros, add the water and butter to a saucepan and bring to the boil. Add the flour and salt, and beat for 2–3 minutes, until the mixture comes away from the sides of the pan. Remove from the heat and stir in the eggs.

2 Transfer the mixture to a piping bag with a large star-shaped nozzle and pipe 15cm/6-inch lengths on to a baking tray lined with greaseproof paper. Place in the fridge for about 1 hour to rest.

3 While the churros are resting, toss together the sugar and cinnamon in a shallow bowl. Set aside.

4 To make the chocolate sauce, add both chocolates, the golden syrup, chipotle chilli flakes and sea-salt flakes to a heatproof bowl. Warm the cream in a small saucepan until steaming, then pour it over the chocolate mixture and stir to combine. Pour the sauce back into the saucepan and set aside off the heat.

5 Heat the air fryer to 180°C/350°F.

6 To get the churros in the air-fryer basket, cut the greaseproof paper around the churros, so each is on an individual piece of greaseproof paper. Carefully transfer these to the air-fryer basket, leaving plenty of space between them.

7 Cook for 18–20 minutes, until crisp and golden (do this in batches, depending on the size or your air fryer).

8 While the churros are cooking, gently reheat the chocolate sauce.

9 When the churros are ready, toss them (still warm) in the cinnamon sugar. Then serve these up ready for everyone to get messy and dip away with the chocolate sauce. Be prepared to clean some mucky faces!

MY SUGGESTIONS

Caramel sauce (see page 179) to dip into makes a sweet alternative, or leave the churros as they are and enjoy them nice and warm with no sauce at all.

Serves 4–6 (makes lots)

250ml/1 cup water
75g/5 tablespoons butter
125g/1 cup plain/all purpose flour, sifted
pinch of salt
3 eggs
2 tablespoons golden caster/superfine sugar
½ teaspoon ground cinnamon

For the chocolate sauce
50g/2oz 70% dark chocolate
50g/2oz milk chocolate
1 tablespoon golden syrup
pinch of chipotle chilli flakes (or more to taste)
pinch of sea-salt flakes
100ml/7 tablespoons double/heavy cream

INDIVIDUAL STICKY TOFFEE PUDDINGS

This is my step-dad Jim's favourite dessert, so I had to make sure this one is up to scratch in the air fryer. Just like the delicious bakes and cakes in this chapter, a sticky toffee sponge cooks up perfectly, and when doused in that delicious toffee sauce, we're in heaven.

1 Put your dates in a jug and pour over the boiling water. Leave them to rehydrate for 10 minutes.

2 Heat the air fryer to 170°C/340°F.

3 In a stand mixer fitted with the paddle attachment or with a hand whisk, cream together the butter and sugar until pale and super-fluffy. Add the golden syrup, eggs, orange zest and vanilla and beat until combined.

4 Add the bicarbonate of soda and the orange juice to the rehydrated dates and, using a hand blender, blend together to make a paste.

5 Pour this paste into your cake batter and mix together gently until combined.

6 In three parts, add the flour to the batter, until smooth, then transfer the mixture into individual baking dishes that will fit in your air fryer. Bake for 25 minutes, until cooked through and deliciously sticky.

7 Meanwhile, make your toffee sauce. Put the butter, sugar and golden syrup in a saucepan on a medium heat and stir occasionally, making sure none of the sugar burns, until melted and combined.

8 Once the sugar has dissolved and the mixture is slowly bubbling, add the double cream and orange juice. Whisk the toffee sauce until fully combined and leave on a low heat until thickened – keep stirring it from time to time to prevent it catching.

9 Once the puddings are ready and out of the air fryer, using a skewer or something similar, poke small holes all over the cakes.

10 Pour over half of your toffee sauce so that it sinks all the way into your spongey puddings.

MY SUGGESTIONS

Serve these up with the remaining toffee sauce, and lashings of cream, custard, or ice cream – whatever you fancy, really.

Serves 4

150g/6 large pitted Medjool dates
100ml/7 tablespoons boiling water
120g/½ cup slightly salted butter, softened
125g/⅔ cup light brown soft sugar
3 tablespoons golden syrup
2 eggs, beaten
2 oranges, zested and juiced
1 teaspoon vanilla extract
1 teaspoon bicarbonate of soda/baking soda
150g/1 cup plus 2 tablespoons self-raising flour

For the toffee sauce
100g/7 tablespoons slightly salted butter
150g/¾ cup dark muscovado sugar
3 tablespoons golden syrup
200ml/generous ¾ cup double/heavy cream
2 oranges, juiced

CINNAMON ROLLS

Saucy, cinnamony, sugary rolls. I'm a big advocate of delicious rolls – so much so I've decided to carry a good few around with me day-to-day. I can't wait for you to have that moment when you open the air fryer drawer and just see these beauties looking back at you. What a way to start the day!

1 Melt the butter and milk together in a saucepan. Remove the pan from the heat and allow the mixture to cool to body temperature.

2 Mix the flour, salt, sugar and crushed cardamom seeds together in a large bowl, then sprinkle over the yeast.

3 Whisk 1 egg into the milk and butter mixture, then pour the mix into the bowl of a stand mixer with a dough hook attached. With the mixer running slowly, gradually add the dry ingredients, then increase the speed and knead for 10–15 minutes, until shiny and elastic. Cover the dough with a damp tea towel and leave to rise for an hour, or until doubled in size.

4 To make the filling, mix together the butter, sugar and cinnamon and set aside.

5 Line a baking tray that can fit in your air fryer with greaseproof paper.

6 Tip the dough on to a lightly floured surface and roll it out into a rectangle, about 20 x 30cm/8 x 12 inches. Spread the filling evenly over the dough, then, starting at the long edge, roll up the dough tightly into a cylinder. Trim the ends and discard the trimmings, then cut into 12 equal slices, each about 3cm/1¼ inches wide. Turn the slices so that they are spiral upwards, place on the baking tray and cover with a clean tea towel. Leave the rolls to rise for 30 minutes, or until doubled in size.

7 Heat the air fryer to 160°C/325°F.

8 Lightly whisk the remaining egg and use it to brush the buns then place them in the air-fryer basket (on or off the baking tray, depending how they fit) and bake for 25–30 minutes, until golden (check the rolls halfway through – if they are browning too much, cover with foil). Remove from the oven and allow to cool for 10 minutes or so, before placing on a wire rack and leaving to cool.

9 To make the icing, gradually mix the water into the icing sugar, adding more or less water as required, until pourable but not runny. Drizzle the icing over the buns using a spoon or piping bag.

Makes 12

*75g/5 tablespoons
  unsalted butter*
250ml/1 cup whole milk
*450g/3⅔ cups strong
  white bread flour,
  sifted, plus extra for
  dusting*
1 teaspoon salt
*50g/¼ cup golden
  caster/superfine
  sugar*
*12 cardamom pods,
  seeds removed
  and crushed*
*5g/scant ½ teaspoon
  fast-action yeast*
2 eggs

For the filling
*100g/7 tablespoons
  unsalted butter,
  softened*
*50g/¼ cup golden
  caster/superfine
  sugar*
*1 tablespoon ground
  cinnamon*

For the icing
1 tablespoon water
*100g/1⅓ cup icing sugar,
  sifted*

BANANA FRITTERS

I couldn't write a book without a recipe dedicated to my best friend Martha, who has a life-altering fear of bananas. If you're less fearful, batter them up and get them in the air fryer for a lovely treat at the end of the meal. Dollops of ice cream, too.

1   Heat the air fryer to 180°C/350°F and lay a sheet of greaseproof paper in the air-fryer basket.

2   In a large mixing bowl, stir together the flour, bicarbonate of soda, baking powder and salt. Whisk in the egg, milk and oil until you have a smooth batter.

3   Peel, then cut each banana diagonally into four pieces and toss the pieces through the batter.

4   Sit the fritters on top of the greaseproof paper in the air-fryer basket and cook for 10 minutes, until the batter has set. Remove the greaseproof paper, flip the fritters over in the basket and cook for another 5 minutes, until crisp and golden. Dust with icing sugar, and a pinch of cinnamon, if you wish.

MY SUGGESTIONS

Eat these with vanilla ice cream, drizzle them in double/heavy cream, slather them in chocolate sauce (make the one from the churros recipe on page 201, if you like), pile them up with fresh fruit, or sprinkle them simply with icing sugar.

Serves 4

150g/1 cup plus 2 tablespoons plain/all purpose flour
1 teaspoon bicarbonate of soda/baking soda
1 teaspoon baking powder
pinch of salt
1 egg
150ml/⅔ cup whole milk
2 tablespoons vegetable oil
4 large bananas
icing sugar, for dusting
pinch of ground cinnamon (optional)

EGG CUSTARDS

An egg custard is a grandma's favourite, and rather than picking up a box or two in your local supermarket, try making them at home for a fresh twist on your usual. They're lovely slightly warm too.

1   Heat the air fryer to 130°C/270°F.

2   Whisk together the egg yolks, sugar and salt in a medium mixing bowl. Pour the double cream into a small saucepan and warm until steaming. Allow to cool slightly, then pour the hot cream over the egg mixture and stir to combine to a custard.

3   Pour the custard equally into the tart cases and generously grate with nutmeg. Add the tarts to the air-fryer basket and cook for 8–12 minutes, until just set. Keep a careful eye on them as they will quickly turn from under- to over-baked! Allow to cool to room temperature before serving.

MY SUGGESTIONS

Serve with a nice cuppa while watching an episode of your favourite TV sleuth – now that's a dream Sunday afternoon!

If you need to use larger mini graham cracker pie crusts then this will make around 6 tarts. The baking time may be slightly longer but keep a careful eye on them.

**Makes 18 small or
6 medium tarts**

3 egg yolks
*30g/2½ tablespoons
golden caster/
superfine sugar*
pinch of salt
*165ml/⅔ cup double/
heavy cream*
*18 mini or 6 medium-
sized sweet shortcrust
pastry tartlet cases*
nutmeg, for grating

INDEX

I say potato...

A big hello to everyone in North America! You'll find measurement conversions throughout the book, but I know there are a few words that are a bit different over your way. Below, you'll find a list of Britishisms and what they relate to on your side of the Atlantic.

Aubergine	Eggplant
Back bacon rasher	Thin-cut slice of Canadian bacon
Bacon lardon	Pancetta cubes or thick-cut slices of bacon cut into strips
Banana shallot	Use a regular shallot
Bangers	Sausages
Bap	Soft white bread roll
Beef dripping	Beef tallow
Beef mince	Ground beef
Bicarbonate of soda	Baking soda
Black pudding	Blood sausage
Bourbon biscuit	Chocolate creme sandwich cookie
Bulb of garlic	Head of garlic
Butty	Sandwich
Caster sugar	Superfine sugar
Cavolo nero	Tuscan kale
Chestnut mushrooms	Baby bella or cremini mushrooms
Chicken wing drums	Drumettes
Chicken wing thighs	Flats
Chinese leaf lettuce	Napa cabbage
Chinese-style pancakes	Mandarin pancakes
Chilli	Chili (the dish)
Chilli(es)	Chile(s) (fresh)
Chipolatas	Skinny sausages. Try breakfast links
Chippy	Fish and chip shop
Chips	Fries
Cocoa powder	Unsweetened cocoa powder
Cooking mozzarella	Low-moisture mozzarella cheese block
Coriander	Cilantro (fresh)
Cornflour	Cornstarch
Courgette	Zucchini
Crisps	Potato chips
Crispy shallots	French's crispy fried onions
Custard cream	Vanilla creme sandwich cookies
Dark brown soft sugar	Dark brown sugar
Dark chocolate	Bittersweet chocolate
Dark muscovado sugar	Dark brown sugar

Demerara sugar	Turbinado sugar
Desiccated coconut	Unsweetened shredded coconut
Double cream	Heavy/whipping cream
Double Gloucester cheese	Colby cheese or use extra cheddar
Dried chilli flakes	Crushed red pepper flakes
Extra mature cheddar	Extra sharp cheddar or aged cheddar
Fast-action yeast	Instant yeast
Filo pastry	Phyllo pastry
Flapjack	Oat bar
Flat-leaf parsley	Italian parsley
Gherkins	Dill pickles
Golden caster sugar	Use superfine sugar or Domino golden sugar
Golden syrup	Lyle's golden syrup
Gram flour	Chickpea flour
Green pepper	Green bell pepper
Icing sugar	Confectioners'/powdered sugar
Jacket potato	Baked potato
Joint	Cut of meat
Jumbo oats	Old-fashioned oats
King Edward potatoes	Russet potatoes
King prawns	Extra-large shrimp
Knob of butter	Pat of butter
Lamb mince	Ground lamb
Lamb's lettuce	Corn salad
Light brown soft sugar	Light brown sugar
Longstem broccoli	Broccolini
Mange tout	Snow peas
Maris Piper potatoes	Russet potatoes
New potatoes	Baby white potatoes
Orange pepper	Orange bell pepper
Pak choi	Baby bok choy
Piccalilli	Try mustard pickles as an alternative
Plain flour	All-purpose flour
Pork chop	Bone-in pork loin chop
Pork mince	Ground pork
Prawns	Shrimp
Red chilli	Red chile
Red Leicester cheese	Colby cheese or use extra cheddar
Red pepper	Green bell pepper
Rolled oats	Quick-cooking oats
Rocket	Arugula
Samphire	Sea beans
Sausagemeat	Use breakfast sausage
Sea bass	Branzino
Sea-salt flakes	Flaky sea salt, or use half the amount of fine sea salt
Self-raising flour	A combination of all-purpose flour, baking powder and salt. Make your own with this ratio: 1 cup flour + 1½ teaspoon baking powder
Soured cream	Sour cream

	Spring onions	Scallions/green onions
	Starters	Appetizers
	Stem ginger	Ginger preserved in syrup or use crystallized ginger
	Stock	Broth
	Streaky bacon	Slice of bacon
	Strong white bread flour	Bread flour
	Tatties/spuds	Potatoes
	Tin/tinned	Can/canned
	Tomato purée	Tomato paste
	Turkey breast steak	Turkey breast cutlet
	Turkey crown	Bone-in turkey breast
	Turkey mince	Ground turkey
	Vanilla pod	Vanilla bean
	White cabbage	Green cabbage
	Wholemeal flour	Whole wheat flour
	Yellow pepper	Yellow bell pepper
	Yorkshire pudding	Popovers
Equipment	Baking paper	Parchment paper
	Baking tray	Rimmed baking sheet
	Cling film	Plastic wrap
	Greaseproof paper	Use parchment paper
	Kitchen paper	Paper towels
	Muffin tray	Muffin pan
	Nozzle	Piping tip
	Tea towel	Dish towel
	Tray	Use a quarter or half sheet pan or rimmed baking sheet
Other	Deseeded	Seeded
	Finely sliced	Thinly sliced
	Lashings	Lots of

- Flour, sugar and cocoa cup measures are spooned and leveled.
- Brown sugar measurements are firmly packed.
- Other non-liquid cup measurements are loosely packed.
- Where we have given measurements in cups and in metric weight, please use only one set of measurements.
- Where ingredients are prepared, the cup measures are for the prepared ingredients. For example, ⅓ cup grated cheese or ½ cup chopped herbs or 1 cup sifted confectioners' sugar or ¼ cup chopped chocolate.

A NOTE ON AIR FRYERS AND TOASTER OVENS

An air fryer has a very powerful fan that circulates air around the food and cooks it very quickly. As the recipes in this book have been developed for, and tested in, an air fryer, you will not get the same results if using a toaster oven or convection oven.

Thank you

It truly takes a team to publish a book and I couldn't be more grateful for the fabulous people I've had at my side throughout this whole process.

Firstly, the incredibly talented, foodie extraordinaire Jo Jackson, who I was lucky enough to have working alongside me in testing recipes and food styling on set, as she became equally as passionate as I am about the humble air fryer. Thank you for the help Jo – I hope you'll think of me every time you're air-frying a sausage in future!

Secondly, a huge thanks to the creative team for making everything air fryer just so beautiful. Our photographers Elizabeth Haarala and Max Hamilton took endless photos of potatoes that looked so good I'm considering having them as wallpaper in my house. The props genius Alexander Breeze did an incredible job on styling and somehow managed to make a bulky air fryer look like modern art in some cases (I LOVE THAT CHEESECAKE SHOT!). And thank you to our food assistants Sarah Vassallo and Caitlin Nuala for helping to make some of the gorgeous food on set too.

Thirdly, thank you to everyone at Bloomsbury for their continued support, especially Rowan, Kitty, Emily, Ellen, Shunayna, Isobel and Helen. It's crazy to think about the first time we spoke back in 2020 (shout-out to Holly as well), and how you took a punt on some random unemployed chef making videos online ... to where we are now ... and I can't wait for what's to come either!

It was a pleasure to work alongside my copyeditor Jude Barrett. (Jude, I've just remembered I promised to send you an air fryer and I'd totally forgotten, but please expect that in 3–5 working days. I'd recommend trying the Basque cheesecake first!)

Finally, thank you to my family for putting up with my frantic chapter writing/cooking/testing/rewriting and late-night texts asking them to retry recipes for me just to make sure they were perfect. Thank you to my mom, Vicky, for all your help with everything air fryer and testing recipes last minute. If anyone's not happy with the honey roast carrots though, I'll send them your way. Thank you to my partner, Tom, for trying his best to organise everything coming together and for spell-checking everything to[*].

And I'd like to actively not thank my two incredibly cute pugs, Kipper and Krypto, for constantly distracting me when I should be testing and writing air-fryer recipes. Not cool, lads.

[*] That misspelt 'too' was just to annoy Tom, sorry.

About Poppy

Poppy has spent a decade in professional kitchens – ranging from Michelin-starred restaurants and fine-dining experiences to serving tasty everyday food. In March 2020, while working as a junior sous chef at an exclusive members' club, the Covid-19 pandemic hit and she lost her job. She turned to TikTok as a creative outlet, and her entertaining and educational content led to more than a million followers in just over seven months. She shares the skills she's learned from her time in the restaurant industry to inspire and teach people how to cook at home, from the basics, right up to achievable restaurant-quality food – as well as a potato or two.

Poppy published her first book, *Poppy Cooks: The Food You Need*, in 2021. She has been a judge on E4's *Celebrity Cooking School* and the debut series of BBC's *Young Masterchef*.

Poppy lives in Birmingham with her boyfriend and two pugs.

Find Poppy **@poppycooks** on TikTok
and **@poppy_cooks** on Instagram.

Appetite by Random House® and colophon are registered trademarks of Penguin Random House LLC.

Library and Archives Canada Cataloguing in Publication is available upon request.
ISBN: 978-0-525-61294-0
eBook ISBN: 978-0-525-61295-7

Printed in China

Published in Canada by Appetite by Random House®, a division of Penguin Random House Canada Limited

www.penguinrandomhouse.ca

10 9 8 7 6 5 4 3 2 1

appetite
by RANDOM HOUSE | Penguin
Random House
Canada

FSC
www.fsc.org
MIX
Paper | Supporting
responsible forestry
FSC® C008047

Designer:
Peter Moffat
at Jon Croft Editions

Photographers:
Elizabeth Haarala
and Max Hamilton

Food Stylists:
Poppy O'Toole
and Joanna Jackson

Prop Stylist:
Alexander Breeze

Indexer:
Vanessa Bird